THE INNOVATION PREMIUM

THE INNOVATION PREMIUM

How Next Generation Companies
Are Achieving Peak Performance
and Profitability

RONALD S. JONASH
TOM SOMMERLATTE

PERSEUS PUBLISHING
Cambridge, Massachusetts

A CIP record for this book is available from the Library of Congress.

ISBN: 0-7382-0360-2
Copyright © 1999 by Arthur D. Little, Inc.

Perseus Publishing is a member of the Perseus Books Group.

Text design by Heather Hutchison
Set in 11-point Minion by the Perseus Books Group

Perseus Publishing books are available at special discounts for bulk purchases in the United States by corporations, institutions, and other organizations. For more information, please contact the Special Markets Department at HarperCollins Publishers, 10 East 53rd Street, New York, NY 10022, or call 1–212–207–7528.

Find us on the World Wide Web at http://www.perseuspublishing.com

1 2 3 4 5 6 7 8 9 10—03 02 01 00
First paperback printing, November 2000

We would like to dedicate this book to our clients and colleagues, whose tremendous insight and experience helped make it possible.

CONTENTS

● ●

ACKNOWLEDGMENTS

· ·

This book is the fourth in a series of Arthur D. Little books on critical technology and innovation management issues. These books include *Breakthroughs, Third Generation R&D,* and *Product Juggernauts,* and our first set of acknowledgments go to the trailblazing efforts of those authors: John Ketteringham, Ran Nayak, Phil Roussel, Kamal Saad, Jean-Philippe Deschamps, and Tamara Erickson, and especially to Phil and Jean-Philippe, who provided so much encouragement for this book.

The Innovation Premium is based in large part on the collective experiences of many companies that are innovation trailblazers in their own industries. We would especially like to thank those who have shared their experiences with us for this book, including, Nokia (especially Kaj Lindén, senior vice president), DaimlerChrysler (especially Tom Moore, vice president, liberty and technical affairs), Alcoa (especially Frank Lederman, vice president and chief technical officer, and Greg Smith, former director of strategy and planning, Alcoa Technical Center), British Petroleum (especially David Jenkins, chief technology officer [retired in September 1998], Chris Clarke, team leader in oil management [retired], and Atul Arya, group planning manager), and Canon (especially Dr. Ichiro Endo, managing director and chief executive of product development).

Major emerging best practices featured in this book have also arisen out of the Arthur D. Little series of Best of the Best Colloquia on Technology and Innovation Management, where senior executives from leading companies across industries have shared their hard-won knowledge and lessons learned. We want to acknowledge the importance of their ideas and experiences for this book.

Many of the key themes and findings are substantiated by Arthur D. Little's continuing research in technology and innovation. We thank the sponsors and leaders of these research efforts for their diligence, dedication, and generosity in sharing their insights.

We also wish to express our gratitude to the following: Strategic Technology Leveraging research, sponsored by the *Economist* and led by Michael Moynihan, in addition to the authors of this book; ADL Global Innovation Surveys, led by Robert Crooker, Frank Morris, Richard Granger, and John Collins; ADL research on the correlation of shareholder returns and business valuation with innovation leadership, led by Michael Baltay and Andrew Kinross; ADL Investor/Analyst surveys, led by Michael Baltay, Jay Maclaughlin, and Brian Kenny.

Special appreciation goes to our contributing editors at Arthur D. Little, particularly Nils Bohlin, Michael Baltay, and Frederik van Oene, whose insight and passion for the topic crystallized our thinking and made the book more powerful, and to Brian Kenny, who skillfully managed the team while never losing sight of the finish line.

Thanks also for valuable contributions from Cees Bijl, William Boardman, David Boger, Robert Crooker, Homer Hagedorn, Brian Kenny, Phil Metz, Frank Morris, Andrew Olmsted, Iason Onassis, Mehmet Rona, Robert Shelton, John Walker, and Al Wechsler; for the stalwart efforts of our loyal support staff, particularly Mary O'Brien, Ellen Maguire, and Christopher Schmitt; and for the continuing support of our partners at Wordworks, Inc., especially Christina Braun, Donna Carpenter, Maurice Coyle, Ruth Hlavacek, Susannah Ketchum, Martha Lawler, Edward McPherson, Toni Porcelli, Saul Wisnia, and G. Patton Wright. And special thanks go to our editor at Perseus Books, Nick Phillipson, for his guidance (and patience) throughout this prolonged project.

Finally, a special appreciation to the tolerance and support of the family of Tom Sommerlatte (wife Christine and eleven children—Sven, Tina, Brice, Iris, Mia, Eva, Sara, Eric, Alice, Tommie, and Anna) and the family of Ron Jonash (wife Karen Sobin and six children—Benjamin, Lindsay, Adam, Katie, Eric, and Andrew). It's not very often that two authors have the opportunity to thank such large extended families!

INTRODUCTION

....

Wall Street increasingly places a higher value on innovation than on any other approach to generating bottom- and top-line growth.

More than a change of leadership, more than a merger or an acquisition, more than a renewed commitment to cost reduction, investors consistently reward—and pay a premium for—innovation. We call this the *innovation premium.*

Innovation boosts a company's earnings, speeds growth, ensures an advantage over competitors, and appeals to shareholders. Put another way, businesses that deliver earnings growth based on a continuous stream of new products and services and new ways of doing business capture the innovation premium.

The research supports our argument. When *Fortune* magazine began ranking companies by innovation fifteen years ago, we began examining its findings to see how they correlated with shareholder return. We found strong evidence of the innovation premium in almost every industry. In fact, the *Fortune* data revealed that Wall Street pays attention to even the promise of new products and services.

- The companies in the top 20 percent of *Fortune*'s ratings enjoy *double* the future shareholder returns of the other companies in their industries.
- The companies in the bottom 20 percent report shareholder returns that are *less than a third* of the other companies in their industries.

Encouraged by these initial findings, we conducted a survey of Wall Street analysts. We discovered the following:

- Some 95 percent of Wall Street analysts responding to a recent Arthur D. Little survey report that the more innovative companies enjoy a share-price premium over their less innovative counterparts.
- More than 90 percent report that the importance of innovation has increased significantly over the last ten years.
- More than 70 percent say that innovation is a key driver of how the market values companies.

How do innovative companies innovate?

That was the question that spurred us to launch a 700-company worldwide study on the innovation premium and its roots.

- More than 84 percent of the senior management respondents report that innovation is now a significant strategic issue for their businesses.
- More than 49 percent of our respondents reported progress in developing and applying systematic measurement and management practices to innovation at their businesses, but they cited a considerable gap in the effectiveness of current practices.

Given the value of the innovation premium, we were surprised to find that fully 85 percent of the 700 companies surveyed were dissatisfied with the way they managed innovation. So to help them develop and manage innovation throughout their organizations, we offer *The Innovation Premium*.

This book points the way toward a more flexible, faster-response business model—a next-generation model—in which companies move beyond continual improvement, total quality, and reengineering and recognize innovation as the key driver of sustainable top- and bottom-line growth. The tenets of next-generation innovation management have been road-tested by some of the world's largest and most successful companies, including Alcoa, Boston Scientific, British Petroleum, Canon, Eveready Battery Company's Energizer unit, Millennium Pharmaceuticals Inc., Chrysler (now Daimler-Chrysler), Hilti, Nokia, Pfizer, and Sun Microsystems, all of which you will read about in the pages that follow. These companies span all sorts of industries, not necessarily those that earmark huge sums of money for research and development. They also have an amazing resilience in the face of market adversities and demonstrate a can-do attitude in their support of creativity and invention.

In contrast, many of their competitors seem stuck on a treadmill. They often operate according to the traditional business model, which recognizes research and development as a prime driver of economic value but keeps it on a tight leash, focused on immediate business, market, and manufacturing needs. It costs too much money, advocates of this outmoded approach argue, and a research and development team, if left to its own devices, can become an entity that speaks to no one, answers to no one, and doesn't know what anyone wants for the company.

The traditional research-and-development department—particularly in the aftermath of reengineering and downsizing—acts as part of a product-development process ruled by budgets and head counts. And when researchers are viewed as a cost rather than as an asset or investment, they begin to spend their days cranking out variations of old products instead of dreaming up new ones. The future takes a back seat. Indeed, this attitude toward research and development figures prominently in what our colleagues at Arthur D. Little call first- and second-generation management, in which companies look upon research and product development simply as an overhead cost, whether centrally managed or driven at the level of the business unit.

During the early 1990s most companies moved beyond isolated R&D management to integrate it with marketing, manufacturing, and other critical business functions. Moving to what our colleagues dubbed third-generation R&D management, companies no longer sever the research and development arm from the rest of the organization, isolating—or, in some cases, protecting—it from contaminating influences. In the third generation, research and development becomes, in effect, part and parcel of the whole enterprise, a primary director of the company's strategy and culture.

In *The Innovation Premium* we carry this argument to its next logical step—the focus shifts from research and development management within a company or business unit to *innovation* management across the extended enterprise, including customers, suppliers, and strategic partners.

We offer next-generation innovation management not as a theoretical exercise—a project to stimulate blue-sky thinking about the what-ifs of the years ahead—but as the focus of immediate concern for any manager who wants to see his or her company succeed.

Next-generation methods beckon companies to venture forth to a new territory where they can

- create and capture new value in new ways
- spark new products, services, processes, and businesses
- create new rules and opportunities for competitive advantage and breakthrough outcomes

The road to the next generation is clear. The journey leads beyond traditional product development to seamless innovation from concept to customer, beyond well-aligned research-and-development strategy to robust innovation strategy, beyond a quarter-by-quarter mentality to a focus on sustainable growth and value, and beyond cross-functional project teams to enterprise-wide innovation networks.

The next-generation approach is not a single breakthrough that creates value and growth. Nor is it the mule that simply grunts and pulls a carriage. Rather, it is a high-performance engine powered by the four cylinders of strategy, process, resources, organization, and based upon a foundation of continuous change and learning. It is sparked by an adventurous spirit and a farsighted vision that is not distracted by the proximity of the next milestone.

Managers with next-generation vision see all the way to Wall Street and Fleet Street, where investors are cheering earnings potential for the future, not just cost reductions for today. They are also positioned to reap the innovation premium with their customers, creating high-value products and services and strong customer loyalty and brand equity. They are positioned to capture the innovation premium with employees, generating higher recruiting yields and strong workplace morale. They are positioned to capture the innovation premium with partners, establishing strong supplier preferences and alliances.

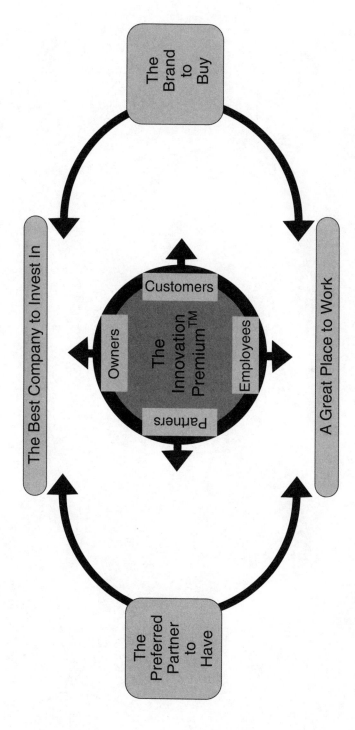

Business Innovation creates and captures premiums across all a company's stakeholders, including shareholders, customers, employees and partners.

FIGURE 1.1 Creating and capturing innovation premiums for all your stakeholders
Source: Arthur D. Little, Inc.

THE INNOVATION PREMIUM

MEET THE
NEXT GENERATION

••

Alcoa, British Petroleum,
Canon, Chrysler,
Lucent Technologies, and Nokia

The term *business cycle* is a misnomer. As we know all too well, there is nothing cyclical or predictable about the rate of economic growth. The good times may last months or years; they may reach historic heights or plateau early. Ditto for the bad times.

Until the early twentieth century, economists did little more than describe the business cycle and wring their hands over its excesses. Then a number of intellectuals, Joseph Alois Schumpeter among them, began a search for tools that governments might use to maintain the rises and cushion the falls—to keep the business cycle's fluctuations within bounds. They came up with the basic monetary and fiscal policies that are still wielded today, particularly when the markets, in the words of a Cole Porter lyric, get "too hot not to cool down."

A professor of economics at Harvard University until his death in 1950, Schumpeter identified and described the essential contribution that innovation makes to economic growth. As he saw it, innovation encompasses the entire process that starts with an idea and continues along through all the steps from initial development to a marketable product or service that changes the economy. Schumpeter would have found support for his thesis in such relatively recent and extraordinary innovations as the jet plane, the personal computer, and high-definition television. Each is an "invention," but each also represents much more than the creation of a new device or product.

True innovation, as we argue in this book, is the driving force not only of individual companies but also of entire economies. To thrive amid ever-fiercer competition, companies and their managers must realign strategies, processes, resources—indeed, entire organizations—to focus directly on innovation and one of its key enablers, technology.

Like Schumpeter, we use the word *innovation* in its broadest sense, including everything that goes into the creation of new products, services, and processes, start to finish. Standard research and development, as productive as some companies make it, is inadequate to this task. In fact, we believe that the traditional view of research and development, typical of what we call first-generation R&D management, is one of the biggest obstacles to any company's attempt to innovate, attract capital, and grow.

ENTER THE NEXT GENERATION

In contrast to the limited approach of functional excellence embodied in first-generation R&D management, the next-generation business model operates on two fundamental principles.

First, a company's managers must *drive innovation across the entire extended enterprise to create value.* In any organization geared to robust idea generation and concept development and fast, flexible responses to business challenges, it is essential to accelerate learning, build cross-enterprise networks, and expect real-time expertise. Within this environment, the skills and capabilities of individual employees can be aligned with a particular challenge on a project-by-project basis. Furthermore, because dozens of permanent, cross-disciplined networks are linked, their members, whatever their current assignment, can be tapped to work on special projects that fit their skills and experience.

True innovation never occurs in isolation. Whether it is learning how a new idea can be incorporated into a full-blown project or how a technique or best practice can revolutionize an entire department's view of its work, that learning animates the next-generation model. If allowed to flourish, learning becomes the force that inspires all of the company's stakeholders, from suppliers to end users.

The second fundamental principle of next-generation management is: *to leverage technology and competency to drive sustainable innovation and capture competitive advantage.* The next-generation model requires the construction of what we call technology and competency platforms, made up of a powerful blend of human skills, competencies, and state-of-the-art technologies, which can be tapped to drive powerful growth and innovation engines and significant improvements in both top-line and bottom-line performance.

These platforms might include, for example, the expert systems at a leading pulp and paper company or the traction systems at Daimler-Chrysler's railroad rolling stock business, ADtrans. Working from sophisticated technology platforms, developers at Millennium Pharmaceuticals, Inc., engage in gene mapping and produce a broad range of scientific compounds. Similarly, researchers at Alcoa profit from broad-based technology platforms used in the creation of new alloys. Canon, Inc., builds competence platforms to improve digital imaging and to share with its business partners the fruits of new discoveries. Boston Scientific builds its next-generation platforms around leading-edge plastic-extrusion capabilities. In each case a technology and competency platform is designed specifically to support and drive the growth of a given portfolio of innovations.

To activate these two principles and achieve the objectives of next-generation innovation, a company needs to align and fine-tune its management efforts in five key areas: strategy, process, resources, organization, and learning. By alignment we mean that all stakeholders in the company—from suppliers to stockholders to end users of the company's products and services—must be involved in and committed to the company's program for innovation. Think of an internal-combustion engine in which all parts are so well tuned that the engine purrs along in one smooth and efficient operation. To extend the metaphor, think of the cylinders of that engine as representing the five key areas of strategy, process, resources, organization, and learning.

Let's take a closer look at each of these five areas, which we consider the pathways to the innovation premium.

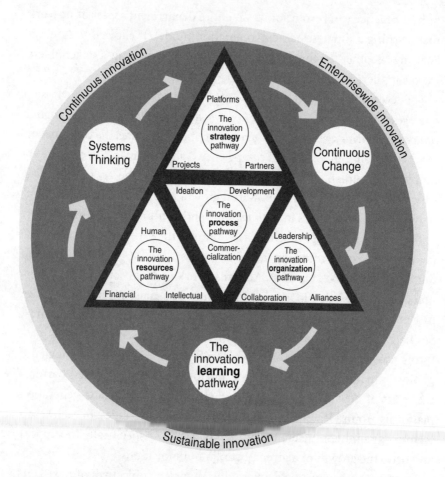

FIGURE 1.1. Next-generation high-performance innovation framework

What Is Next-Generation Innovation Strategy?

Traditionally, the perceptions and goals of major business units—marketing, production, and the like—have determined business strategy. More recently, corporate cost reduction and restructuring priorities, as well as mergers and acquisition opportunities, have also driven those strategies. Today, more than ever, as companies strive to grow *both* the top and bottom line, innovation has moved to the forefront as a key strategic driver. A next-generation innovation strategy is fully aligned with the company's strategic vision and is tailored to the needs and strengths of a company's innovation-and-technology apparatus, and that of its extended enterprise of partners, suppliers, and customers.

Who's on the Pathway to Next-Generation Innovation Strategy?

"A lone wolf among Japanese companies" is how the media have characterized Canon. The company has shied away from the traditional interlocking *keiretsu* relationships with big banks and other corporations. Its treatment of employees also runs counter to custom. For one thing, Canon introduced the five-day workweek to Japan. And instead of developing spin-offs of others' products, a favorite tactic of Japanese companies, Canon relies upon its own researchers and business innovations to break new ground.

The results have been extraordinary. Canon has leapfrogged from cameras to copiers to computer peripherals (such as scanners and printers) to technical products (such as steppers for the semiconductor industry). For years the company has been among the top five recipients of patents in the United States, and many of them have been category-killers. Profits have soared, reaching almost $1 billion a year in 1997 on revenues of $21 billion.

Canon's success is directly tied to its innovation strategy. The company makes no bones about it: "Advanced technology development and innovation is at the heart of our strategic thrust," says Toru Takahashi, director and chief executive of the company's research-and-development headquarters in Tokyo.

In subsequent chapters we will show in greater detail how strategy has figured in Canon's success. The company is well on its way to becoming a next-generation model for others to emulate, and the assessment of Wall Street supports that conclusion.

What Is Next-Generation Innovation Process?

In the traditional view product development begins with research and development and ends with a hot-off-the-assembly-line product or service. As a step toward next-generation management, we urge people to expand their thinking to include the entire process, from the point of origin of raw ideas to the point at which the product is in the hands of a loyal customer and the intricate system of feedback loops in between.

Think, too, of the new and more efficient techniques that a company puts into the hands and minds of its employees. Where do such techniques come from? They might come from anywhere in the company's value chain—from competitors or even from other industries that may have been using the techniques in a different context for decades.

Who's on the Pathway to Next-Generation Innovation Process?

The Nokia Corporation shows how an expanded perspective can take the process beyond the day-to-day demands of a single business unit and enhance value for the long term. For a decade this Finnish conglomerate floundered as sales in its paper, rubber, and telecommunications divisions steadily eroded. The breakup of the Soviet Union, the company's major market, increased its anxiety and losses, a whopping $200 million for 1991 and for 1992.

Then to the astonishment of the business community, Jorma Ollila, Nokia's chief executive officer, bet the company's future on a single market: telecommunications. Today, Nokia is the largest in worldwide mobile phone sales, having recorded annual revenues of $15.7 billion in 1998. And the company is outdistancing all comers in maintaining its technological lead in so-called smart phones.

Nearly unknown in the United States until a few years ago, Nokia is now a brand to be reckoned with. Indeed, the company has become a source of thoroughly innovative products. How did it happen? Nokia redesigned its innovation process. "In the past," says Kaj Lindén, former senior vice president of technology at Nokia, "we were very much engineering-driven. Research and development was a separate and sovereign entity pursuing its own esoteric goals, and the company simply awaited the results of this group's activities."

In a redesign of the old R&D process, however, Nokia engineers were introduced to their end-use customers and to the realities of the marketplace. "We learned to understand that the new emphasis would be on time to market," Lindén says, "that the earlier you're in the market, the more control and profits you are able to garner." For the first time in any systematic way, the engineers were also introduced to the exigencies and logistics of production, and to the needs and capabilities of Nokia's suppliers. They learned to share ideas and information across the whole enterprise and to operate through multifunctional teams and technology and innovation platforms. In essence, they learned to innovate.

A stream of new ideas is produced by a research-and-development staff that numbers 8,000—out of a total workforce of 34,000. But everyone is involved in the innovation process at Nokia, where ideas are just the beginning of business insight and wisdom. When market conditions demand, the people at Nokia can launch a new product from a standing start in no more than six weeks. This extraordinary performance level will be at the center of discussion in Chapter 4.

What Are Next-Generation Innovation Resources?

The next-generation model enlarges the definition of business innovation resources to include all of the capital, facilities, capabilities, and people that are part of or connected to the innovation process. Customers and suppliers are definitely on board. Managers need to determine whether and how to leverage these resources to drive innovation.

Who's on the Pathway to Next-Generation Innovation Resources?

When Chrysler was facing possible bankruptcy in the 1980s, it lacked the financial capital to support its research-and-development resources. Mere survival required some innovative thinking on how best to use what resources the company had. Management at all levels began taking a hard look at every possible source of research and production, in effect redefining what the term *resources* meant. By viewing the company as an extended enterprise—in part by wooing its suppliers and winning their loyalty—Chrysler was able to turn near demise into bonanza. Today, one in every six vehicles sold in the United States is a Chrysler product, and some 85 percent of all automotive suppliers consider Chrysler their preferred customer.

In years past carmakers in the United States were vertically integrated, manufacturing nearly every part of the vehicles they sold. Suppliers were treated like second-class citizens, expected to compete on price and delivery for every scrap from the Big Three's table. Contracts were short, and the relationship between assembler and supplier was, to put it mildly, at arm's length.

When necessity forced Chrysler to rethink its research-and-development and innovation structures, the company totally recast its relationship with suppliers and began treating them as an essential part of its extended enterprise. It offered them the assurance of long-term contracts as well as the price incentives to become allies, if not partners. Supplier experts were invited to join Chrysler's vehicle-platform teams, which are made up of engineers, designers, and factory personnel.

Accepting the invitation, Chrysler's suppliers responded by sharing their own new technologies with Chrysler. Those supplier/Chrysler teams are an integral element of the company's innovation process.

To achieve its objectives, Chrysler has at times upended automotive tradition. For one thing, the company now shares knowledge of its operations across its extended enterprise. "Ford and General Motors work hard to keep their cards close to their chests, so to speak," according to Tom Moore, general manager for Chrysler's Advanced Technology Division. "What we do is entirely the opposite." Before Chrysler designers, engineers, and executives even know what a new vehicle will look like or how it will function, the suppliers are brought in as partners. "We explain the total vehicle philosophy," Moore says. "Suppliers can then see how the part they are supplying interfaces with other parts."

That kind of team involvement encourages the participation expected of a partner and is far removed from the old hired-hand approach. The arrangement not only offers suppliers many benefits, but it also gives Chrysler much-needed access to the innovation resources of its suppliers, as we will see particularly in Chapter 5.

What Is Next-Generation Innovation Organization?

The next-generation company builds a highly collaborative organization from the top down and the bottom up, one that is thoroughly networked in ways that enable people to communicate rapidly with one another. By connecting workers at every level and in every corner of the organization and beyond, next-generation managers encourage the personal interactions and cross-fertilization that foster innovation. An idea that pops into one worker's head can be shared with colleagues and teased into becoming a new project. A newly devised manufacturing technique in one department is passed on to the whole enterprise. A best practice garnered from a partner or a technical paper is extended to all stakeholders in the value chain.

Managing this interaction and cross-fertilization, a company's chief development officer (CDO) is responsible for inspiring, fostering, and riding herd on company-wide innovation and technology. The CDO also shoulders the responsibility for developing new businesses and technologies, formulating technology and product strategies, and building and exploiting intellectual property. On the executive level, the CDO is assisted by innovation and development boards and councils. On the day-to-day level, the officer's mission is supported by permanent technology and competency networks made up of specialists from across the supply chain who can be called on to lead innovation projects. The CDO also builds and energizes alliances with innovative outside organizations and individuals.

Who's on the Pathway to Next-Generation Innovation Organization?

Alcoa—originally known as the Aluminum Corporation of America—encompasses a diverse range of companies and business units with a large research and development component. The parent company, despite being in an industry largely perceived to be commodity driven, has made innovation synonymous with the name. It is famous for bringing aluminum beverage cans to the packaging industry, the aluminum space frame to the automobile industry, and a multitude of advanced alloys to the aerospace industry. Besides reaching for wide product diversity, Alcoa embraced an ambitious strategy to extend its enterprise globally and to improve communications and manufacturing techniques while also attempting to cut production costs and inventories.

Recognizing the impossibility of realizing such a strategy if the company continued to function in discrete, hierarchically structured silos—

where the production and sharing of knowledge and innovation were hindered by the word *proprietary*—Alcoa's leaders undertook an equally ambitious plan to streamline the organization and to ensure that processes and people worked seamlessly together. Their journey is the subject of Chapter 6.

Dr. Greg Smith, former director of strategy and planning at Alcoa's Technical Center near Pittsburgh, Pennsylvania, points out that merely downsizing or instituting various measures to ensure continuous improvement would not have been sufficient in themselves to bring the company up to next-generation status. He believes that closing the technology gaps—both internally and across the extended enterprise—depends on a networked and team-oriented approach for the entire organization.

What Is Next-Generation Innovation Learning?

Above all, the next-generation company is a dynamic, knowledge-based learning machine, committed to continuous and sustainable innovation. That, too, requires the leadership of the CDO, who might as easily be called the CLO, chief learning officer. The electronic network is organized to gather ideas and best practices from every corner of the company, to select and edit them, to send the newly polished versions back to the desks and workstations where they can be put to practical use.

Who's on the Pathway to Next-Generation Innovation Learning?

The companywide learning that takes place at the London-based British Petroleum Company (BP) shows that such a network can be a tremendous asset. BP officials credit a powerful learning program for the dramatic turnaround achieved by this $71-billion global giant over the last decade. The old BP was an unwieldy, extremely diversified organization, with major stakes in coal, oil, natural gas, and various minerals. Its exploration and development costs were among the industry's highest, and by the early 1990s corporate indebtedness had reached an all-time high of $16 billion.

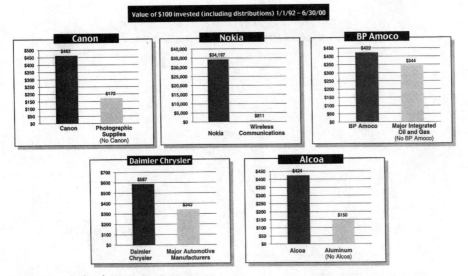

FIGURE 1.2 Who has the Innovation Premium
Source: Media General Financial Services and Tradeline®/Dow Jones Interactive (Nokia only).

Since then, BP has reduced both its workforce and its debt by half and become the most profitable of all the major oil companies. In its turn-around, BP has relied on units it calls performance improvement teams, which incorporate elements of various networks, each responsible for one of three primary assets: learning, competence building, or performance improvement.

In many companies, especially those with a first-generation mentality, the time that employees spend in dialogue and in reflection is often seen as a wasted effort. But at a next-generation company such as BP, just the opposite is true. As Chris Clarke, former team leader in BP Oil Management, puts it, "A great deal of effort is focused on getting people to reflect and learn from what they've done. It's valuable experience."

One of the values BP has derived from this learning is the importance of a corporate culture built on teamwork. Workers are strongly encouraged to move beyond a focus on their particular personal or departmental concerns and to treat all teammates as collaborators in a common cause. "We reward how well people work with others," says Atul Arya, group planning manager at BP. "One of the criteria for moving up to more senior levels in the organization is how well you deliver on that particular metric."

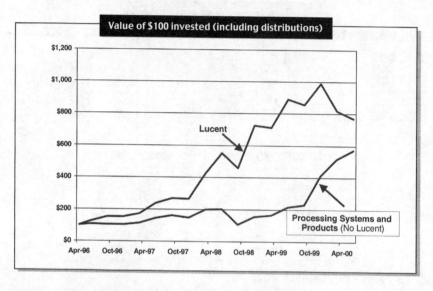

FIGURE 1.3   Lucent shareholder returns vs. industry average, 1996-2000
Source: Media General Financial Services.
Note: Lucent stock began trading on April 4, 1996.

The Peer Assist Program is one tool BP uses to teach teamwork and the larger view. Instead of bringing in experts to solve team problems, they rely on peers to resolve problems. We will examine this environment for continuous change and learning in Chapter 7, which focuses on how companies such as British Petroleum build a culture that supports continuous learning as they move to next-generation status.

Although the companies in this chapter have emphasized different pathways to next-generation innovation management, each continues to progress in all five key areas of strategy, process, resources, organization and learning. These companies have already captured a substantial innovation premium, as demonstrated in Figure 1.2.

Putting It All Together

Few companies can match Lucent Technologies in producing innovative products and sustaining the energy of that innovation. Since parent AT&T spun off Lucent in 1996, the new entity has accrued an impressive list of innovations such as the digital subscriber line (DSL) modem chip, which offers Internet connections up to twenty-five times faster than a typical 56K modem. And a recent announcement disclosed Lucent's plan to put its HomeStar Wiring System in 55,000 new houses scheduled to be built in Las Vegas, Nevada; Gilbert, Arizona; and Miramar, Florida. These houses will feature high-tech wiring systems for telephones, fax machines, personal computers, entertainment equipment, and video-surveillance systems, all of which appeal to homeowners eager to be digitally equipped for the next millennium.

In a demonstration of both growth and profitability, Lucent has compiled a record that is the envy of its competitors. And it continues to capture value that translates into rewards for all its stakeholders. (Lucent's stock price shot up more than 160 percent in 1998 alone.)

The company spends 12 percent of its annual revenues on research and development, a healthy allocation of resources. That translated to an outlay of more than $3 billion in 1997, based on revenues of more than $26 billion. Lucent has its own venture-capital fund, which seeks out companies with innovative technologies that will complement the Lucent product line. And as we will explore more fully in Chapter 5, the company leverages its assets and resources in ways that enable it to manage the decisions about whether to make, buy, or collaborate in the production of innovations it needs. Lucent, in short, is an innovation pathfinder, a company that is putting strategy, process, resources, organization, and learning together to reach next-generation status.

Although the companies in this chapter have emphasized different pathways to next-generation innovation management, each continues to progress in all five key areas of strategy, process, resources, organization, and learning. These companies have already captured a substantial innovation premium, which will be discussed in more detail in the chapters ahead.

2

THE PROBLEMS OF
BUSINESS AND
MANAGEMENT TODAY

What Used to Work So Well
No Longer Does

Venturing into new management territory can be daunting. The old haunts are familiar and comfortable—and, besides, they've worked fine for generations despite short-term thinking, turf wars, and fear of conflict—just to name a few of the most obvious drawbacks. But the problem is that the old haunts are also limiting. Remaining huddled inside them limits access to new realms of growth and value and does nothing to cope with the whole new set of circumstances facing business today.

To be sure, many of us are prone to stay with the routine and avoid change. Fortunately, we have other characteristics that counter our inertia. Pride in achievement, a thirst for knowledge, and the will to succeed are some of the inner forces that drive us to enter new territories. The same stimuli also spur next-generation enterprises looking for ways to achieve advantage. The advantage may be only temporary, but successful companies learn how to capture it and then move on to the next opportunity.

It is getting harder and harder to replicate this scenario in today's business environment, however. Here's why:

1. *Intellectual property is becoming increasingly difficult to protect and preserve, measure and manage.*

As the economy shifts from a product-based system to a knowledge-based one, managers need ways to manage their investments in intangible assets that drive innovation. Keeping intellectual property or any kind of secret secure in this era of the Internet, high staff mobility, and open communication has become very difficult. And maintaining the loyalty of smart employees is a problem of major proportions.

Witness the furor created when General Motors lost its top purchasing chief, Jose Ignacio Lopez de Arriortua, to Volkswagen. Lawsuits were filed claiming that Lopez stole company secrets, plans, and parts' price lists. The company further alleged that Volkswagen, having hired Lopez and gained access to GM's proprietary knowledge, was able to squeeze $3.5 billion out of its cost structure.

Similarly, consider the difficulties and expenses that many companies incur in pursuing patent and copyright infringement suits in the developed world, let alone in less-developed regions. It is no wonder, then, that many business leaders, who view innovation only as a patent portfolio or some other form of intellectual property, consider it to be a risky and unsecured investment that is extraordinarily difficult to value or manage.

2. *Businesses—even entire industries—are no longer insulated from the competition, and innovation leadership is difficult to sustain.*

Mergers and acquisitions continue to vault from peak to peak. What was once thought to be extraordinary, the record $600 billion of mergers consummated in 1989, was far eclipsed by the more than $2 trillion of M&A activity in 1998. It marked the seventh consecutive year of merger increases.

Furthermore, worldwide competition has forced many markets and manufacturers to relocate and consolidate in the never-ending search for ways to cut costs. A company can no longer hide behind the fortress of a vertically integrated organization, ignoring the strategies and processes of its competitors. As boundaries collapse and benchmarking and industrial espionage increase, many business leaders see innovation as one of the most valuable assets they possess in their quest for weapons to achieve sustainable competitive advantage.

Innovative cultures cannot escape the impact of these competitive pressures, especially when a merger seeks to bring together two radically different environments. Culture clash was evident in the October 1997 union of NationsBank Corporation of Charlotte, North Carolina, and Montgomery Securities L.L.C. of San Francisco, California.

Before its merger with Bank of America, NationsBank paid $1.2 billion for Montgomery Securities, an investment bank known for its involvement in the fast-growing high-tech and telecommunications industries. Montgomery's founder and chief executive officer, Thomas Weisel, wanted to maintain his own vision and strategy for managing specific areas such as high-yield bonds and equity investments. But NationsBank's top officials, known for being more conservative, were intent on incorporating the entrepreneurial firm's prior management methods only insofar as they were in sync with NationsBank's entire franchise. Not surprisingly, this arrangement was deemed unproductive by Weisel, who resigned in September 1998.

3. *The nature of competition itself has shifted to cost leadership in many industries, and reengineering-driven cost reductions have overwhelmed many innovation initiatives.*

From the fast-food industry to the manufacture of automobiles and televisions, reengineering-driven cost-cutting measures have become the favored quick fix. Reverse engineering, on the other hand, has sometimes made it difficult for business leaders to substantially differentiate their products and services from those of their competitors. In this environment company managers might well look upon innovation as impractical, expensive, and thus of limited value.

Short-term solutions such as reengineering, downsizing, and outsourcing can, indeed, help cut costs, and reverse engineering can often make you a fast follower. But these strategies frequently work to the detriment of innovation. Rarely do such measures inspire long-term thinking about what the company does best, what ambitions it wants to achieve, and how best to get to its destination.

4. *Technological advances have radically altered the old view of research-and-development techniques, leaving many traditional R&D departments mired in yesterday's key competences and technologies.*

Just as the word processor has forever changed the way we think about writing, fast-paced technological change in industries as diverse as pharmaceuticals and space exploration has caused people to think differently about research and development. Moving incrementally from one product to another or making small improvements in this year's model over last year's can no longer keep a company competitive and sustain its innovation program.

New products and services are the lifeblood of business, whether you are the Miller Brewing Company, which now collects 90 percent of its total revenues from beers that did not exist two years ago, or Millennium Pharmaceuticals, which collects much of its revenues from products that aren't even on the market yet. The continuing shrinkage of product life cycles leads Nathan Myhrvold, the coauthor, with Bill Gates, of *The Road Ahead*, to warn that however good a product may be, it's probably not going to last in its current form for more than eighteen months.

Yet many traditional R&D departments remain mired in the technologies of yesterday and the base competences inherited from the past. They are tied to line extensions ordered up by marketing departments and incremental improvements ordered up by operations departments. They are unwilling or unable to look at potentially disruptive technologies and breakthroughs.

5. *Traditional research-and-development managers focus primarily on internal operations, while the extended enterprise, which includes suppliers, partners, and customers, often remains unmanaged.*

In the post-reengineering world managers have treated research and development as just another overhead cost, a narrow view that has reinforced a circle-the-wagons mindset in some R&D operations and other shared services. R&D managers often do not share the company's overview of all its resources across the extended enterprise of outside partners and sources.

The innovation premium is about working smarter rather than simply working harder. Faced with the pressures we have outlined above, companies must become faster and more versatile. We are not suggesting, however, that you must dramatically restructure your company's entire strategy, reorganize all your resources, or completely change your processes and organizational structure. What we do suggest are ways to alter your approach and overlay new management practices that can create and capture more value from innovation.

This is a job for managers—your job—but before you can tackle it effectively, you need to understand the problems plaguing today's accepted management techniques. Many business managers and their counterparts in research and development are pursuing innovation approaches that are stalling. Why? Because traditionally conceived research and development can no longer be the prime engine of value and growth.

There are four words that every manager of traditional research and development can repeat even in sleep: *hurry up and invent.* The word order of that imperative is instructive, for it suggests that speed is actually more important for most managers than is the thing invented. If you don't believe that, try to remember the last time you heard an R&D manager say, "Invent! Oh, yes, and can you be quick about it?"

Under the old dispensation of tight budgets, huge risks, and market threats, an innovative product could fall flat as a failed soufflé at any point in the cooking process. Managing research and development required a master chef who could keep an eye on many boiling pots at once.

To begin with, corporate management had to be convinced that funding some unproven product would pay off, if and when someone found a yet-undiscovered audience. Marketing managers had to be persuaded to consult the oracles in hopes of determining a future demand for an as-yet-uninvented product. Researchers and developers, meanwhile, had to be prodded into thinking up the invention that would be the company's salvation and make Wall Street take notice. Build a better mousetrap, the product developers were told, but do it before the mice wise up.

R&D managers have always had their share of problems in securing resources, finding the talent, and balancing priorities somewhere between the extremes of unbridled freedom and the need for on-time, on-budget product and service innovations. Without direct control of budgets, they have had to parcel out meager resources, determining who will do the inventing and how it will be done but rarely how much will be adequate. Moreover, managers have been hampered by being out of sync with the organization's overall strategy: Should the researchers and developers work to come up with products that will fit with what marketers think will be needed five years from now? Or should the marketers accept the responsibility of finding (or building) the audience needed to buy the product that the researchers have created?

Such questions have long perplexed not just manufacturers, but artists and producers, too. In 1997, for example, CBS launched seven new shows in its fall lineup, not one of which survived the first season. And the other major networks did not fare much better: only six of the thirty-six shows first aired that fall found audiences large enough to justify continuing production.

Television shows that fail in their initial launch fall into the category of "products all dressed up with no place to go." So, too, does a Polaroid Corporation failure that occurred in the late 1970s, when the company invested $70 million in an instant home movie system called Polavision. It was part of a strategy to develop proprietary technology in a line of products that Polaroid hoped would take a bite out of Kodak's huge market share. But Polavision proved to be toothless, and its failure contributed to the company's shift to a strategic focus on marketing rather than product innovation. That decision ultimately led to Edwin Land's 1982 retirement as Polaroid's CEO.

Although R&D managers face a plethora of problems, the biggest one, we believe, is expressed in the subtitle of this chapter: "What Used to Work So Well No Longer Does." And what is it that no longer works? One thing that does not work is having R&D managers who are concerned primarily with what takes place within the four walls of the corporate headquarters and the local facilities responsible for developing and manufacturing the product. This approach, typical of a first-generation enterprises, focuses on *internal* operations, and the company looks upon research and development as an overhead cost, whether centralized or decentralized. First-generation organizations often resort to "management by intuition"—that is, with both technology and the demand for it uncertain, R&D managers must rely on a gut reaction. What's more, when it comes to setting objectives, doling out resources, and fulfilling expectations, the company's general management has its own agenda, which the managers of the R&D functional departments often do not share.

Although second-generation R&D operations become broader-based as the recognition dawns that there must be a strong connection between the work of the innovators and the business itself, the managerial focus is still restricted to internal operations. Thus, everyone's attention remains riveted on the product—a product that may or may not have much relevance to the company's overall business strategy.

This fledgling spirit of cooperation becomes more pronounced in the third-generation company, which integrates the R&D function across the enterprise to an unprecedented degree. There is a new spirit of partnership and trust with general management, and research and development is perceived as something more than just an overhead cost. But although R&D is no longer locked away in the most isolated reaches of the facility, the spotlight still shines unwaveringly on the tangible *product*.

We believe that the next-generation enterprise has to reexamine its definition of product, however, and recognize it as something much more inclusive than just the better mousetrap or the sitcom that scores a hit with this season's television audience. The next-generation enterprise no longer directs all its efforts toward inventing a product in hopes that an audience will buy it.

The individual product or service is still important, to be sure, but it no longer occupies the center of corporate attention. Next-generation managers must learn to speak a new language that advocates fluid and nimble product and business development, able to adapt at a moment's notice to new opportunities in marketing, financing, processing, and skills development. What's more, the product no longer needs to be tangible, with immediately practical applications. Next-generation R&D is adept at recognizing the potential of any piece of information, any innovation, any new skill that arises. Knowledge creation is recognized as an invaluable asset, for example, as is a customer's suggestion for continual improvement or a supplier's contributions to a tired process.

SET THE PACE
∙∙—

Build Platforms, Not Just Products

Canon, Inc., may indeed be "a lone wolf among Japanese companies," as the media are wont to describe it; it has largely avoided joining Japan's historically powerful *keiretsu* business coalitions. Neither does it follow the pack when it comes to turning out new products: Canon prefers to mine its own original ideas rather than borrow inspiration from competitors.

Despite its go-it-alone image, the company has mastered the art of developing strong partnerships to shore up areas in which it lacks expertise. And therein lies the secret of its next-generation success. Canon's innovation strategy combines a commitment to creating new platforms for growth and innovation with a willingness to find new partners to secure leadership in those platforms.

And it's no wonder that investors like what they see, too: the returns to Canon's shareholders have far exceeded the industry average and the overall Japanese market (see Figure 3–1).

When the company was founded in 1933 as the Precision Optical Instruments Laboratory, its goal was to produce Japan's first 35-mm camera. The product was originally called the Kwanon (for the Buddhist goddess of mercy); the brand name Canon was adopted later. Among Kwanon's meanings is "standard for judgment," deemed suitable for a precision industry. At the outset the company focused its core capabilities on optics and gave its researchers the time and resources needed to bring new discoveries and patents to fruition. Today, it devotes 10 percent of its sales—

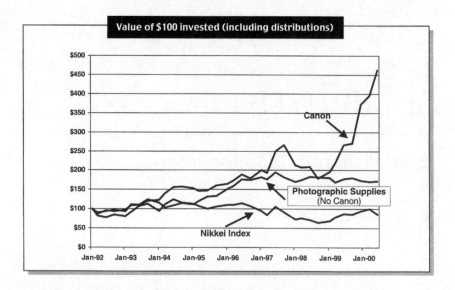

FIGURE 3.1   Canon shareholder returns vs. industry average, 1992–2000
Source: Media General Financial Services, Tradeline®/Dow Jones Interactive (Nikkei Average).

about $1.5 billion each year—to innovation-oriented research and development.

In 1962 Canon managers adopted the company's first five-year plan aimed at diversifying in preparation to enter the business machine market. In the field of plain-paper copying, it appeared that Xerox had a corner on the market, with an overwhelming 600 patents on related technology. However, Canon's leaders were intent on competing despite the fact that the patents made it impossible to copy the invention. What's more, Xerox was unwilling to license it.

Six years later, Canon unveiled its revolutionary NP plain-paper copier technology and in 1972 launched the world's first liquid-dry copier. Then it moved into laser printers and fax machines. Today, only about 8 percent of the company's sales come from cameras, while copiers and printers account for about one-third each.

Toshiba and other competitors might opt to produce bread-and-butter commodity items such as computer chips, but Canon has never been interested. All along, Canon has bet on its ability to leverage the company's key capabilities in order to come up with advanced concepts that can be turned into high-margin products.

Case in point: the copier saga. At the same time the company was developing and launching its plain-paper copier (PPC), it was creating the liquid-dry plain-paper copier in compact size and the dry one-component PPC. Each, in turn, gobbled up market share from its predecessor. "We have no fear of cannibalism," says Toru Takahashi, director and chief executive of the company's research and development headquarters in Tokyo. Indeed, Canon's introduction of the BubbleJet® printer, while its laser-beam printers were still on top of the heap, proves the point.

Nevertheless, it is a risky and costly strategy that requires high levels of discipline and dedication from company managers and workers. And it is not without its pitfalls. For example, being technologically independent, as Canon has sought to be, has it advantages, but focusing on its core capabilities has sometimes left the company weaker in other technical areas. Consequently, Canon has had to develop aggressive partnering strategies.

Some years ago, for example, company scientists came up with the idea for a high-speed digital copier with a charge-coupled device (CCD) sensor. Existing sensors were inadequate, and Canon had not developed a strong sensor capability. So the company convinced Toshiba to help create a better sensor. The result of this joint venture was a new and better copier. Furthermore, under a codevelopment contract, Canon received exclusive rights to the Toshiba piece of the product for two years. Only after this time was Toshiba free to sell its product elsewhere.

Canon's approach starts from the traditional assumption that a strong business strategy is essential—that research-and-development projects must be aligned with business priorities and the needs of individual business units. But then the company's strategy goes beyond that well-recognized insight and into our next-generation model.

DEFINING NEXT-GENERATION INNOVATION STRATEGY

Next-Generation Innovation Strategy Is About Platforms

Lone wolves tend to be hungry wolves. Unlike many of its Japanese counterparts, Canon does not roam in others' territory, however. Rather than develop knockoffs or extensions of its own or competitors' products,

Canon has always based its strategy on finding new wellsprings of innovation—the *platforms* we described in Chapter 1.

Platforms originated in the car industry. At General Motors and Ford, Volkswagen/Audi, Mercedes-Benz, and others, the growing number of models and types—each engineered by separate development groups for separate marketing or sales divisions—led to rocketing development costs and a staggering array of diverse parts, components, and technical solutions, not to mention duplication of knowledge and effort.

The platform concept was originally aimed at imposing a common chassis on an entire family of cars so that development efforts could be concentrated on optimizing the traction system, power train, axles, transmission, braking system, and so forth. Car manufacturers were thus able to broaden their competence in the development of the now-common platform technologies, reduce logistical costs, and speed up the introduction of new models.

We have transfered the product platform concept to apply to any bundled set of key technologies or competancies that can be developed and applied as the basis for growth and innovation in a variety of products and services. The needed technologies or competancies are often relatively difficult to develop, but, once acquired and bundled they represent a tremendous competitive advantage over companies that do not have all of them.

Not only "chassis" technologies, but also manufacturing methods and know-how, application expertise, systems capabilities, a vision of how platforms will evolve and open up new opportunities in the future—all of these belong to a platform. It is critical to both recognize key platform components and manage them strategically. You also have to have the imagination and flexibility to maximize the innovations that come from them.

Platform Levels

In next-generation enterprises, platforms are often virtual or informal structures, loose coalitions of people roughly organized around particular areas of expertise. When devising next-generation strategy, one must identify and characterize these platforms according to four specific management approaches, or levels. Each level demands a different degree of management control, investment, and strategic alignment, generally escalating to the most intense attention and largest expenditure at level four.

A level-one platform, which we designate as *knowledge and learning*, might encompass an area about which you know little and want to know more. It might prove to be promising for innovations, but you need a knowledge and learning platform in order to make that judgment. In other words, this level is exploratory or tangential. It requires less management control, lower investment, and a looser alignment with strategy.

Level two, what we call *excellence and leadership-building* platforms, describes structures often formed in response to a situation—say, a trend or a developing technology or a change in customer need—that looks as if it will have an impact on a company's business. It's not yet clear what that impact might be, but management knows it has to monitor the situation. And to stay ahead of the game, it chooses to work toward a leadership position by becoming very good at something. Doing this obviously takes greater attention from management and a larger commitment of resources.

At level three, *innovation and development* platforms, management recognizes that this area of expertise is the epicenter of a good deal of creation and innovation. A continuous stream of new products and services will definitely come out of this platform, and the company is investing heavily to make it happen. The organization is actively managing the unambiguous potential for innovations at this level and establishing clear accountability for top- and bottom-line results.

Level four, *business-performance and growth* platforms, defines an area that is already turning out a successful product or service and intends both to continue developing products and to defend its position in the face of competition from others. This level has demonstrated business value, clear accountability for tangible growth or improvement, and a highly orchestrated and motivated team. It is only one step below an independent business entity with its own formal organizational structure.

The four platform levels are a critical area for next-generation strategic choice. Leaders recognize that not all areas of expertise command the degree of management commitment needed to bring them to level four. And determining how much attention and resources an area receives will require an assessment of other strategy components, such as partnerships, customers, and markets. It is a decision that cannot be made in isolation.

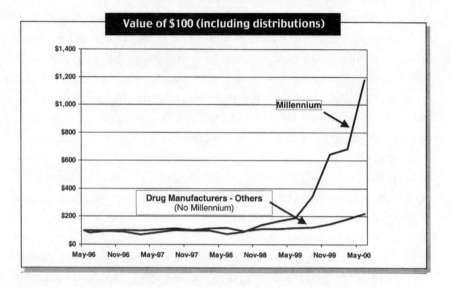

FIGURE 3.2   Millennium Pharmaceuticals vs. industry average, 1996–2000
Source: Microsoft Investor, Arthur D. Little Analysis.

Next-Generation Strategy Is Also About Innovative Partnerships

Sometimes platforms are not enough. Just as when Canon had no platform dedicated to sensors and entered a joint venture with Toshiba, next-generation strategy often depends on a portfolio of strong partnerships. Millennium Pharmaceuticals, Inc., of Cambridge, Massachusetts, ably demonstrates the power of partnerships in a next-generation strategy.

Millennium is a leading-edge drug-discovery and -development company. It has wisely used multiple collaborations to propel itself from a start-up in 1993 to an influential player in the notoriously precarious biotechnology industry. What was once a team of thirty researchers has grown into a company of more than seven hundred top-flight scientists, managers, and technicians. This elite group works in genomics—the study of genes and the part they play in certain diseases—and has produced early leads in the treatment and diagnosis of conditions such as obesity, asthma, and central nervous system disorders.

What sets Millennium apart from other biotech companies—indeed, from most companies of all kinds—is the structure and focus of its corporate strategy. Millennium leaders recognize that this strategy must cultivate innovation in core technologies and key sources, partnerships, and alliances. It is not focused single-mindedly on producing, producing, producing. Millennium's leaders faithfully adhere to the mantra that all next-generation players should follow: We do not have products, we have shareholders.

In fact, so compelling is Millennium's strategy that its leaders have been able to drive hard bargains when negotiating alliances with powerhouses such as Monsanto, Eli Lilly and Company, Hoffmann-LaRoche, Inc., and Bayer AG. In nearly all its partnership arrangements to date, Millennium has extracted hundreds of millions of dollars from collaborators in return for drug discovery, targets and leads, and technology transfer services. But what is most striking about these deals is that Millennium retains the rights to use the knowledge generated by this process for itself in a wide range of complementary—occasionally even competitive—areas.

In the partnership with Eli Lilly, for example, Lilly helps fund Millennium's research into therapeutic proteins. Millennium qualifies the candidate proteins to a pre-clinical stage. Every three months both companies examine the "pool" of proteins discovered and divide them up equally in order to develop them further. Even though Eli Lilly provides significant funding for the project, Millennium still retains control and selling rights for 50 percent of the discoveries.

As Millennium's chief technology development officer, Michael Pavia, Ph.D., explains, "We get more money from downstream partners than most other companies because people recognize us as a premium player. They're happy to pay the premium." The company is a premium player not only because of what it is today but because it is continuously developing cutting-edge expertise. "They pay us more, and we're able to deliver, so that just builds on itself," Pavia adds.

At the heart of Millennium's rapid growth and uncommon success is Mark Levin, the company's founder and chief executive officer. Levin sees the biotech business not in traditional terms, as a purely scientific search for a compound, but rather as a complex production process in which both science *and* technology have starring roles.

In trying to make the discovery chain as efficient as possible, Levin and the Millennium organization draw on a multitude of technologies ranging from robotics to information systems, which are then wrapped into a package with molecular biology to create an innovative, integrated science and technology platform. The goal is to speed up the process of sifting through the estimated 100,000 genes that carry instructions for making a human being and to identify those that are associated with disease.

Companies such as Millennium that establish strong and meaningful partnerships with downstream and upstream players, not to mention customers, begin to function, in effect, as extended enterprises. As sophisticated as their technology may be, most of these companies have concluded that they simply cannot do it alone: delivering value to customers and shareholders requires the cooperative work of too many people, too many business groups. Companies reap great benefits by developing deeper and broader partnerships that can promote innovation across the entire extended enterprise.

In Millennium's case, for example, a cross-fertilized portfolio of partnerships translates into a two-way transfer of technology and value. The company uses such transfers both to realize immediate value from its investment in technology development and to augment the resources available for such development.

A case in point is Millennium's alliance with Monsanto. Monsanto has gained access to state-of-the-art genomics technologies for use in plant and dairy agriculture, whereas Millennium is able to leverage its integrated science and technology platform for agriculture. The five-year, $218-million deal will fund more than a hundred scientists and bring Millennium's genomics technology to a new Monsanto subsidiary. The purpose of Millennium's partnering strategy is to give it access to partners "who will take the fruits of our platforms and drive them forward, providing the financing to expand these platforms further," says Steven Holtzman, the company's chief business officer.

Similarly, other deals have given Millennium access to technology developed by other firms. In fact, CEO Levin has been called the Mao Zedong of biotech, eager to buy or use other people's technology to facilitate what he believes should be a continuous revolution in both technology and organization. The company has a team of people dedicated to hunting for partnerships around the world.

Millennium has relentlessly pursued this aspect of next-generation innovation. Recently, it entered into one of the most highly priced alliances ever forged in the drug-discovery field. Bayer AG, the German chemical and pharmaceuticals giant best known for its aspirin and One-a-Day vitamins, agreed to pay Millennium $369 million for five-year access to its aggressive drug-discovery research programs. In addition, Bayer will invest an extra $96 million to obtain a 14 percent interest in Millennium.

Millennium's role in this alliance is to continue its work in the area of genomics research, using the technology it has developed. That technology enables researchers to sift more quickly and easily through hundreds of thousands of the proteins expressed by human genes in their search for suitable drug targets.

Over the next five years, Millennium will supply Bayer with 225 drug targets that may be useful in designing drugs to treat specific diseases such as cancer, osteoporosis, cardiovascular, liver fibrosis, pain, hematology, and viral infections. Bayer has the right to select as many as 10 percent of these proteins for potential development into drugs. If any of the drugs make it to market, Bayer will pay royalties to Millennium. Furthermore, Millennium will retain the rights to the other 90 percent of the discovered proteins and will be free either to develop them into drugs itself or sell them to a third party.

This approach exemplifies Millennium's innovation strategy by allowing it to sell a narrow application of its technology for a large amount of money. The Bayer arrangement also leaves Millennium free to establish other alliances in unrelated disease areas on top of the more than $500 million in collaborations it already has with Monsanto, Pfizer, and Eli Lilly, among others.

Millennium is experiencing the exponential and sustainable growth that the next-generation model is capable of delivering. The company's revenues nearly tripled from the end of 1996 to the end of 1997, and it is one of only a handful of start-ups to break even in its first five years of operation. Wall Street, too, has recognized that the value of a company such as Millennium is based on the innovative interplay of partners and platforms, processes and technologies.

ARE YOU READY FOR A NEXT-GENERATION STRATEGY?

Change Your Mindset

In recent years many companies have focused on aggressive cost reduction and on mergers and acquisitions to close gaps and drive both growth and improved performance. Process redesign has generally been dedicated to reengineering, overhead cost-cutting, and capturing the cost-saving synergies promised by consolidation and post-merger integration measures.

But the goal of next-generation innovation strategy is to move beyond this state of diminishing returns. A new realm beckons in which strategies promote sustainable growth and productivity improvements, leading to strong innovation premiums with customers, employees, suppliers, and shareholders.

Next-generation innovation strategy is far more than research, development, and engineering projects designed to carry out a business plan within the confines of a specific budget (as characterized on the left side of Figure 3.4. See page 35.). This is not to say that available financial resources—and the projects and programs targeted to receive them—don't matter. Of course they do. When it comes down to it, money always matters. But the tail should not wag the dog. In other words, your strategy should determine how your company spends its money, not the other way round (as shown on the right side of Figure 3.4. See page 35.).

Think beyond annual budget plans and the limitations of internal resource allocation. You can view strategy in its true light, as a broad, value-based investment in sustainable growth and performance improvement. To achieve the success of a company like Millennium, you must think like its leaders: "There is no such thing as a cost. Everything is an investment," says Millennium's Pavia.

See Where You Stand

How do you begin setting a next-generation innovation strategy? Ask yourself the following questions:

- Are the company's platforms and product portfolios robust enough to make shareholders confident that the company can continue to innovate?

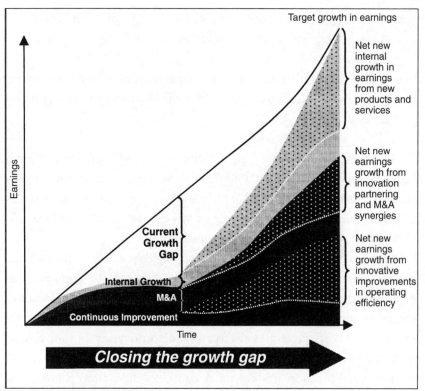

Next-generation companies are focusing on technology and innovation strategies to close the widening growth and performance gap.

FIGURE 3.3 Closing the growth gap through strategic innovation
Source: Arthur D. Little, Inc.

- Are continual improvement initiatives going to gain competitive advantage, or will they be enough only to keep pace with aggressive, cost-cutting competitors and the subsequent erosion of prices?
- What is the average life span of a research and development effort?
- How long can a research and development effort continue without a successful product or service launch?
- Are new cost-reduction breakthroughs necessary and possible?
- Are merger-and-acquisition initiatives sufficient to close critical gaps, or are cost synergies too few and strategic synergies too elusive to justify the high-priced premiums required?
- How are research and development projects funded? How are their budgets evaluated and measured? How are their costs reported?

- How often does the company roll out new products or services? What percentage of revenue or profit comes from new products and services?
- Do new partnering and sourcing opportunities offer better value propositions than those offered by traditional mergers and acquisitions?

Most managers, when carrying out this review, will discover two things. First, the existing strategy as it applies to research and development projects is limited and short-term. It lacks sufficient emphasis on the sources of innovation, and it lacks the long-term view required to facilitate sustainability and breakthrough opportunities.

Second, many find that their existing strategy considers innovation initiatives to be a cost rather than an investment. Research, development, and engineering projects may all be in line with specific business-unit strategies and budget priorities, but the perception that they and their management are a "cost" precludes enterprisewide innovation initiatives and major breakthroughs.

The typical business strategy today considers innovation primarily in terms of research and development, making sure that the various research portfolios are supporting the company's various business priorities. There is no innovation strategy per se; thus, the organization inevitably fails to realize its full potential.

FOLLOW THE PATHWAY TO NEXT-GENERATION INNOVATION STRATEGY

Develop Effective Analytical Tools to Assess Key Strengths, Weaknesses, Opportunities, and Threats

Sure, SWOT analysis has been around for a while, but keep in mind that to be truly effective it must be done across the entire extended enterprise, not just within a business unit or functional department. These tools must be employed in ways that identify key gaps and offer strategies to close those gaps.

Next-generation companies clarify their vision for innovation and build strategies around technology and innovation.

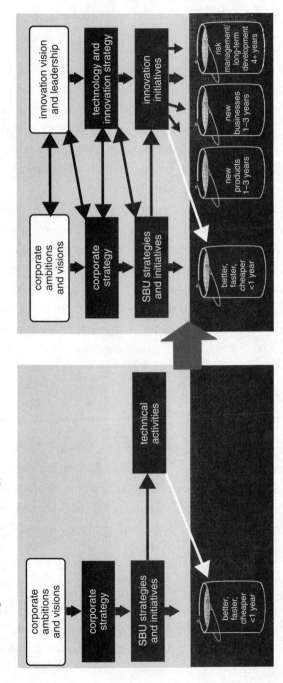

These companies are establishing a balance between better/faster/cheaper initiatives and long-term growth initiatives to drive new products and new businesses.

FIGURE 3.4   How next-generation companies are creating an ambition-driven innovation strategy
Source: Arthur D. Little, Inc.

Develop Road Maps of Emerging Technologies and Business Opportunities, and a Clear View of Alternative Futures

Be prepared to look everywhere—in the ranks of employees, partners, and suppliers, in universities, and in journals—for hints, signposts, and insights. Reading these signs will suggest what fields you should be entering or leaving and what technologies you should be buying or phasing out. Although these resources are important for managing incremental growth and progress in established businesses, they are even more critical for managing the gray spaces across the businesses, the white spaces in between, and the clear spaces of future businesses.

In order to construct your road maps, therefore, you will need to create potential scenarios of what the future looks like and what key drivers or enablers will get you to that future. For instance, will the government pass a bill requiring further emissions cutbacks or the one setting new telecommunications standards? If so, how will the competitive environment in your industry be altered? Is your biggest competitor about to launch its latest innovation? How will that change the demand for your own somewhat different but parallel product now in development?

Prepare Contingency Plans and Set Forth Responses to Potential Scenarios

Should the emissions bill become law, your competitors are likely to stop production. You need to decide now which way you'll jump so you can get ready for that possibility. Should your competitor's new product appear before your own product is launched, it could easily cut demand for your product by 25 percent. You need to have a plan ready to cope with these possibilities.

Establish a Compelling Innovation Vision Tied to a Clear Strategy

Most companies already have strong vision or mission statements embracing some aspect of innovation. Few have taken it to the next level of clarity by developing a strategy to achieve the vision. Companies like Canon and Millennium Pharmaceuticals have, and the impact of this deeper level of commitment is clear in the value of their portfolios and in the impact of their key management initiatives. The point is that vision is much more than blind ambition. An innovative vision and strategy is both driven by and grounded in the reality of your product and technology platforms, your mix of partners, suppliers, and customers, and your allocation of resources.

Play to Your Strengths

No organization has the resources to pursue all its ideas, so you need to focus your firepower on your core areas of expertise—the core technology and competency platforms that have the most potential for creating a continuous stream of innovations. You need to combine your resources with those of your partners to maximize the potential of those growth and innovation platforms and shore up the areas in which you are not strong. In that regard, Canon, Inc. is a master.

Traditionally, Canon's strategies have been governed by the expertise of its technical leaders. Deeply knowledgeable about the core technologies, they were best able to scan the horizon for future developments and then map out the corporate way forward. But a company decision to move into networking systems is altering that tradition.

The company has made a determined effort to train lower-level technical managers in research-and-development strategy and process improvement. Their contributions to strategy are providing the company with a broader view, not only of the technology universe in general but also of the capacities and potential of internal processes.

Canon is now entering a new world of multimedia networking outside its core technologies. Partnering and collaborating in support of robust and accelerated innovation platforms is thus becoming an ever larger factor in Canon's future. That move is radically changing the way the company goes about devising and implementing its technology and innovation strategy.

Canon's leaders are excited about the company's prospects and not in the least modest about its plans. "We intend to transform the way information is accessed on the network," one company official says. "Our customers will no longer be limited to managing data from a central personal computer. Instead, users will be able to access, capture, store, share, manipulate, distribute, and publish information from peripheral devices,

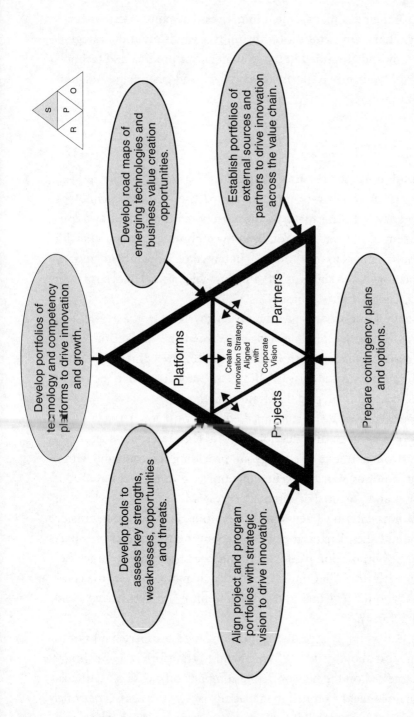

Next-generation companies create an innovation strategy aligned with corporate vision.

FIGURE 3.5   Moving down the pathway to next-generation innovation strategy
Source: Arthur D. Little, Inc.

such as scanners, printers, copiers, facsimiles, and multifunction systems." In other words, Canon is taking on the PC. Although some may scoff at its prospects, a review of Canon's past success with ambition-driven innovation strategy (copiers, scanners, and steppers, for example) should bring skeptics up short.

One recent Canon product is a fine example of its potential in this area: an information-management system that indexes every electronic document in a company's computers. Using it, a company can link together many different documents from within many different programs, such as spreadsheets, Web sites, and reports.

Canon's goal is to create systems instead of simply producing standard look-alike products. The company must therefore respond not simply to the general demands of a mass market but also to the very particular needs of individual customers. The need for customization has put a new premium on market-side intelligence in the creation of company strategy.

Manage Your Portfolio of External Partners and Sources

Turning to outside partners to shore up gaps in your innovation platforms involves more than finding the right fit. Next Generation companies systematically manage their entire array of external technology and innovation sources. Millennium Pharmaceuticals, Sun Microsystems and Chrysler have explicit strategies for how to manage their partners. They have rationalized, consolidated and strengthened their portfolio of partners to become a major part of their innovation strategy.

Align Your Projects with Your Innovation Vision and With Your Platforms and Partners

The hunger for quick paybacks in investments in R&D drives many companies to align their programs and projects with only short-term goals, forsaking the long-term. Next Generation companies have realigned their activities with a richer mix of innovation platforms and partners that build potential for the long-term while still producing results in the short-term. These companies are able to uncover and exploit market opportunities beyond their core markets. They have a revitalized portfolio of projects and programs that reflects a broader insight of the opportunities in and among their existing businesses for the present and the future. Scientists have now had to make room for salespeople at the mapping table.

Clarify Everyone's Roles

It's not enough, of course, simply to gather the requisite pieces and construct a new strategy. Before one can implement a next-generation strategy, one must make clear what everyone's role is in this new milieu. Ensure that the entire organization is committed to both creating and capturing the maximum value from innovation through a comprehensive set of innovation-process improvements, leveraged-resource investments, organization changes, and learning enhancements. In short, the uppermost question in everyone's mind must be: What *exactly* must we do to bring our innovation strategy to life?

KEEP THE PACE

• •

Move Seamlessly from Concept to Customer

Nokia, the world-renowned Finnish telecommunications company, is clearly reaping the benefits of a well-tuned and highly energized next-generation innovation process. It has gone from a struggling conglomerate early in the decade to the largest mobile-phone manufacturer in the world, selling 21.3 million units in 1997.

Red ink and gloomy prospects were the order of the day in 1992, when company leaders boldly launched the entire organization on a costly, high-risk venture. The goal: to produce a portable telephone that could provide access to the Internet, a built-in World Wide Web browser, a calculator, a clock, and the capacity to send E-mail and faxes.

Nokia was no stranger to this burgeoning market, nor was it out of character for the company to reach for the stars. It had a well-earned reputation for introducing cutting-edge technology. Still, at the outset this new venture appeared to be a serious overreach. Nokia was hitching its future to the creation of a product—essentially, a miniature handheld office—that would combine nearly every kind of electronic communication. To achieve its goal, the company needed new technology platforms and new partners, both of which then had to be managed to support a greatly accelerated schedule.

Nokia's leaders relied on a proven product-development process that was driven by a fluid and flexible team drawing on cross-functional resources. But the new wrinkle was in the way the process was dedicated to achieving maximum value from innovation. It was a process that ex-

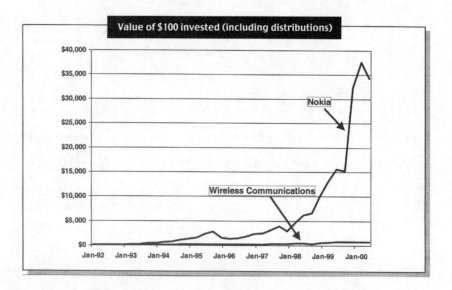

FIGURE 4.1   Nokia Shareholder Returns Versus Industy Average, 1992–2000
Source: Tradeline®/Dow Jones Interactive, Arthur D. Little Analysis.
Note: Stock prices and dividends of Nokia have been converted from their local currency on the Helsinki exchange to U.S. dollars for this comparison.

tended from research and development all the way to end users—a stream we call *concept to customer.*

Nokia's extraordinary success is reflected in myriad ways, not least of which is its return to shareholders. As Figure 4–1 indicates, since 1992 that return has exceeded even its own industry average by more than tenfold.

Even a cursory glance at the all-in-one cellular phone Nokia developed illustrates the fluidity of the next-generation process the company employed: initially code-named Responder, the phone was called the Communicator by the time it landed on store shelves. With a price tag of $1,000, it was top of the line in every way and far ahead of competitor's products.

Taking a cue from Nokia's success, every company interested in achieving sustainable levels of growth needs to incorporate the same kind of fluid, flexible, value-maximizing innovation process.

DEFINING NEXT-GENERATION INNOVATION PROCESS

The next-generation innovation process starts with enriched business concepts, proceeds with speed and flexibility, and ends with high value delivered to a wide range of customers providing explicit feedback for the next generation. This is not the old budget-driven, step-by-step product development or project management process. And it is more than an engineered stage-gate and milestone-based process. It is characterized by seamless innovation from concept to customer, it is a nimble dance across the extended enterprise that begins with the birth of an idea and moves rapidly and flexibly through prototyping, screening, and rollout.

Next-generation innovation is marked by two uncommon features: a wide-open front end in which concepts are varied and plentiful, and a far-reaching down stream in which an array of products and services are rolled out to customers willing to pay a premium for strong, compelling value proportions. Because the beginning of the process drives a search for ideas among a greater variety of sources, it increases the likelihood of finding effective new product and service concepts, methods, ventures, or businesses. The end stage promotes a commercialization process that captures value at every possible point: licensing agreements, patents, and imaginative, often electronic, distribution channels. In this way innovations are exploited to achieve maximum value—whether alone or in partnership with others.

We like to visualize the next-generation innovation process as more a high-velocity venturi tube, as depicted in Figure 4.2. This represents a departure from its typical conceptualization as a funnel, an increasingly restrictive screening process through which concepts are forced.

The first stage of next-generation innovation entails giving idea teams the raw material with which to fashion new concepts as they keep their antennae up to decipher an uncertain future: What new technology is brewing? What new government edicts are in the works? What unmet needs are evident in the marketplace or in the core values of future customers?

The objective is to keep the idea basket constantly filled to overflowing with enriched concepts that speak to both expected and unexpected demands. Those concepts must come from all corners of the extended enterprise—suppliers, customers, distributors, alliance partners, industry groups, university research centers, think tanks, and so on.

Obviously, even some of the best-envisioned concepts will never become products for one reason or another. But Nokia's brimming inventory of product and service ideas means that winners can be quickly pulled down

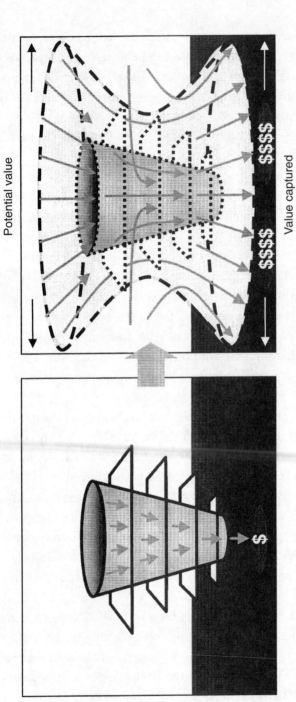

Next-generation companies are using innovation to expand their view of product and technology creation increasing the potential value at the top and the value captured at the bottom, and increasing velocity throughout.

FIGURE 4.2 Creating a seamless and high-velocity innovation process from concept to customer

Source: Arthur D. Little, Inc.

from the shelf in order to establish or maintain a leadership position and expand the company's reach. For example, if a competitor is planning to bring out a new product, Nokia can make a preemptive strike by pushing out its own version to take the edge off the competitor's initiative.

Complexity is a fact of life at the end of the next-generation innovation process. In the typical product development process at most companies, the push is to get the product manufactured, inspected, and out the door to meet the launch deadline and steal a march on the competition. Relatively little time is spent thinking about anything other than the obvious primary market for a product innovation or the primary application for a process innovation. Often, the temptation is simply to hand a new project over to a product or operations manager as soon as possible and move on to the next show.

Because of the enormous energy expended in a successful launch or rollout, many businesspeople believe that they are effective managers of this end of the innovation process. The problem is that nobody bothers to sew up—let alone dream up—all the possible ancillary markets or applications, particularly those that are beyond the scope of a company's current distribution channels or manufacturing operations. At this end of the innovation process, underexploited opportunities often abound.

There are no such regrets at SC Johnson & Son, however. One of the world's largest makers of chemical products for the home, including Windex, Glade air freshener, and Johnson floor wax. The Racine, Wisconsin company has expanded and improved its innovation process to rapidly expand the bottom end of the pipeline: the better to explore new geographical markets. Teams are charged with pursuing agreements that maximize value capture from new product and service innovations.

Similar procedures were put into effect at the Pulp and Paper Research Institute of Canada, commonly known as Paprican, after studies revealed that more than half of the value of the institute's process innovations was being lost, largely because of slow and ineffectual rollout to member mills. Paprican directors and members then moved to focus energy and resources on improving the end of the innovation process. Their efforts paid off; aside from a dramatic increase in tangible returns on its development-process innovations, Paprican saw a significant strengthening of its partnerships across its extended network.

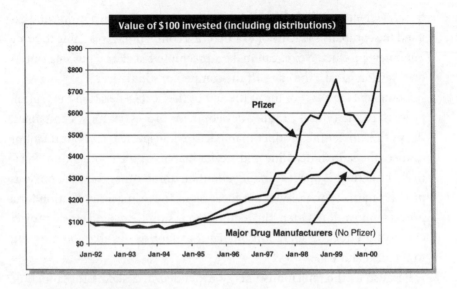

FIGURE 4.3   Pfizer shareholder returns vs. industry average, 1992-2000
Source: Media General Financial Services.

And what lies between the two ends of our innovation process hourglass, between concepts and customers? The answer is speed and flexibility. After all, the innovative insights created in a next-generation enterprise cry out for fast response.

Consider what happened at Pfizer, Inc., the New York-based pharmaceutical company now considered by industry analysts to be one of the top drug companies in the world. For many years, Pfizer scientists researched a drug they believed would treat angina by increasing blood flow to the heart. But by 1992, when the medication still had not shown hoped-for results, plans were made to cancel the project.

Then, the repeated occurrence of one of the drug's side effects caught the attention of scientists working on the project: they discovered that Viagra corrected erectile dysfunction. Managers at Pfizer seized the opportunity to explore this side effect and immediately began clinical trials on the drug's new application.

Six years later the results of Pfizer's quick turnabout produced an astounding success. At Viagra's launch in April 1998 the product rapidly became the fastest-selling new drug in history. In its first full week on the market, 36,000 prescriptions for Viagra were written.

While doing wonders for untold thousands of men, Viagra has also done wonders for the company. From May 1997 to May 1998, Pfizer's market value more than doubled, to $135 billion, far outpacing the performance of the rest of the pharmaceutical industry.

ARE YOU READY FOR THE NEXT-GENERATION INNOVATION PROCESS?

Change Your Mindset

As long as you view product development as a narrowing funnel with strong screening criteria and a dominant mandate of focus, focus, focus, you will continue to emphasize a rigid and over-engineered product-development process that substitutes cost-focused project management for innovation. It's time to stop leaving idea formation to chance and product application to convention.

Embracing the next-generation process requires moving beyond measured and managed product-development procedures and fostering increased flexibility in midstream project management. This new flexibility may generate resistance from employees who have grown accustomed to being measured against the old "on-time, on-budget" metric. But don't be deterred.

See Where You Stand

How do you begin building a next-generation process? Ask yourself the following questions:

- Do you value and manage external input from customers, industry colleagues, and competitors when evaluating your current products or services?
- Do you actively solicit input from these sources in developing new products and services, or is information sharing frowned upon in your company?
- Do you think of the idea people as separate from the real business of making a profit?
- Does your company reward creative idea gathering, idea researching, and successful idea implementation?

- Do your scientists, inventors, engineers, and product creators mix with one another and share ideas with colleagues, both internal and external?
- Do you keep new product or service ideas secret? If so, from whom?
- Do your idea developers keep up with technology and market trends?
- What role do your customers play in product development? Is their input considered merely at the rollout stage, or do you get their opinions, needs, and desires even before an idea is developed?
- When a new idea promises success, how quickly can you move it through your development process?
- Do your product development managers have the authority to speed up, change course, or drop a project altogether?
- What parts of the process do you measure: idea generation, product development, or commercialization?
- Are your project managers free to try new management techniques or different product development tactics?
- What resources—human and financial—do you allocate to the rollout stage of your product development process?
- Do you have employees dedicated to finding new applications for your innovations, as well as new market segments and commercialization opportunities for your products?
- Do you actively search for new ideas and innovations at all stages of development and do you have active licensing, cross-licensing, and co-venturing agreements with other companies, both within and outside of your industry?

Most managers, on conducting this type of review, find that their idea masters are working in a vacuum and that their commercialization people are stuck in a tunnel.

When carrying out this review, you might find yourself hesitating at many of the questions. That could be because you, like most other managers, have concentrated on the middle stage of the innovation process—product development. This stage is obviously easier to manage, and its results are relatively easy to measure.

If your idea-gathering and concept-development stage is stunted, the efficacy of your product-development stage is irrelevant. Many leaders find that those employees responsible for generating ideas are ignorant of market developments, internal expertise, competitor knowledge, and customer preferences. The project handoff between those working in the idea stage, the development stage, and the commercialization stage is just that, a handoff—too often one between a runner and a jogger. There is little or no sharing or updating of information to ensure a smooth process. Moreover, when reviewing product launch procedures, most managers discover a stale, blinkered approach. There is a lack of creative investigation of potential new markets, new customers, and new partnerships.

FOLLOW THE PATHWAY TO NEXT-GENERATION PROCESS

How do you break out of product development and into innovation? Follow these pointers to the next generation.

Exploit the Knowledge and Intelligence of Your Extended Enterprise in Its Entirety

Share knowledge and insights with your company's partners and allies, and observe closely your competitors and what they do. In other words continuously cross-fertilize. Furthermore, you should maintain close relationships with universities and academic researchers, and constantly scan the business horizon for new trends and technologies. In a next-generation enterprise, networking is power, and successfully exploited ideas are shareholder wealth.

Integrate Your Customers and Suppliers into the Innovation Process

Send technical people out to meet with customers to absorb their needs, and integrate lead customers and preferred suppliers into your innovation process through focus groups and brainstorming sessions. If you make an effort to discover what they think of your existing products or services and to determine what it is they really want, what they have to say may sur-

Innovation Vision and Strategy

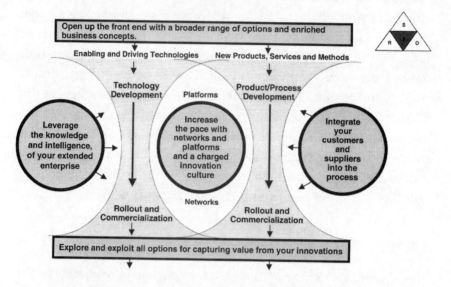

Next-generation companies have pipelines for technology as well as product development. They use platforms and networks to speed information between the two and keep up the pace of innovation.

FIGURE 4.4   Critical pathways to next-generation innovation process

prise you. And those surprises might well spark the next innovative idea your company needs.

Open Up the Front End of Your Innovation Pipelines

You can't afford to have your innovation process thrown off course by its inherently ambiguous beginnings and the difficulty of trying to measure and manage it. Don't forget that the beginning of the process is different on nearly every count from the middle. It covers the areas of ideation, exploration, concept development, and prototyping and typically includes a diverse set of participants and activities until a specific team is established with a project, budgets, and a schedule. This part of the innovation process and pipeline is almost impossible to measure without option pricing and contingency planning. Its results are unclear in the short term, and so is the value of any one particular idea. Typically, only one in five ideas ever makes it to the middle stage, and most of those survivors are themselves eventually discarded.

Many senior managers have little patience with this top-end innovation process; to them, these discarded concepts seem to be simply an enormous waste of time and money. They would much prefer to stand back and insist: "Just pick the winners . . . quickly!" That is easier said than done, of course, although the beginning of the process can, in fact, be managed. The key is to work within the more ambiguous context set by alternative scenarios, contingency plans, options, and insurance policies.

The stream of ideas must be bounded first by the establishment of good criteria as to what is being sought and second by the use of an efficient mechanism to sort and channel what is found. At Hilti AG, for example, leaders recognize that the synthesis of these pathways is the key to reaping the long-term rewards of innovation learning. The Liechtenstein-based Hilti is one of the world's leading producers of fastening and demolition systems for the construction industry. Once merely a small family business, the company now operates in more than a hundred countries and employs 12,000 people. Profits for the Hilti Group were $116 million from January to August 1998, an increase of 13 percent from the previous year.

The main strategic focus at Hilti is on process innovation within product development. The company is renowned for its extensive information-gathering and knowledge-sharing techniques; employees are encouraged to pursue strong ties with strategic research partners and closely observe both competitor actions and trends in the marketplace. The company also maintains extensive customer exposure through its policy of direct sales.

These efforts all contribute to the type of continuous supply of new ideas vital to next-generation processes. The problem, however, was that while Hilti was spreading a wide net for ideas, it lacked a method for sorting the mediocre from the great—the minnows from the marlin, if you like. This meant that all ideas—customer-driven and futuristic, risky and safe—were competing on the same level. Instead of using a rational screening process, managers were being overwhelmed by the profusion of ideas and simply waiting until those with the strongest advocates won out.

Hilti's managers realized that the company needed to combine its proven ability to stimulate innovation with focused strategic guidance. Before promising and profitable ideas could be separated from those that weren't, they knew they had to ask some important questions. For example, in which markets did company managers see growth and differentiation potential? What were the company's core competences upon which to build future product and service offerings? And where did the company have the market strength with which to push innovation?

To answer these questions, Hilti managers created what they refer to as a segmenting program. They now gather together leaders from all areas of the business—planning, development, manufacturing, sales, marketing, and customer service—to determine which segments of the construction industry to work within and which areas are ripe for innovation. They take two questions into consideration: Is the segment large and growing with unmet needs? And does Hilti have the existing or potential strength to do well in this area?

The result of this initiative has been phenomenal. Hilti managers are now able to spot innovative ideas quickly and precisely, and employees can concentrate their attention and creativity on only the most fertile projects that use the company's core areas of competence and expertise. An unwieldy idea development process, fostered by lethargy and opinionated infighting, has been supplanted by an effective and efficient innovation process.

Increase the Pace with Innovation Networks and Platforms

Business moves at ever increasing speeds. So should you. The shelf life for products and services has decreased and the pressures for further cost reductions have grown so much that the very definition of sustainable competitive advantage has changed. Where once such advantage was measured in decades, then years, it is now measured in mere months—and, in some cases, only days. The only way to stay on top is by constantly driving a high-velocity innovation process.

Think of Pfizer. Its "hot-commodity" status in the highly competitive pharmaceutical industry is a fairly recent development. As it began to expand the front end of its innovation process in the late 1980s and early 1990s, however, its innovation rating (relative to the rest of the pharmaceutical industry) dramatically improved.

Starting in 1994, the company's market valuation put it firmly in the lead, in front of the rest of the major pharmaceutical companies. Now, with Viagra capturing everyone's attention and a pipeline chock full of products, Pfizer is being praised by investors and envied by the competition.

So is Nokia, which has risen to previously unimagined heights of fortune on the technology platform of wireless communications, most strikingly with its Communicator technology. But the leaders at Nokia are not complacent. They know that Nokia's competitors are hard on its heels, and they understand the true importance of innovation and its motivating question: "How do we defend our current advantage and find new advantages in our particular business environment?"

Ask Pertinent Questions That Lead to Increased Value from Innovations

As you work to expand the commercialization end of the innovation process, be sure to address the following questions:

- Does your market position allow you to effectively and profitably introduce a new product or service?
- What is the effect of the new development on your product or service line and its evolution?
- Do you have the appropriate manufacturing and logistics capacities, and can you quickly achieve the best economies of scale?
- What is the international market potential of the innovation? Do you have access to a sufficient geographical portion of it?
- What is the value of your innovative solution to other companies in similar as well as very different markets?
- Are There Promising Licensing or Coventuring Opportunities?
- Can the commercialization be pushed effectively through your existing organizational setup or would a spinout, spin-off, or joint venture be more promising?

- Do you have the right people in place to carry the innovation into the market successfully?
- What follow-up resources and efforts will be needed to support and further build the business thrust around the new products/services?

ACCELERATE THE PACE

∙∙∙

Invest in Innovation Platforms and Partners

Within the Chrysler Corporation there exists a unit called Advanced Technology. It is small by most corporate standards, given its very large mandate, which is to develop the concepts for Chrysler cars that will not see the light of day for five or ten years. Company insiders often refer to the unit as the "tip of an iceberg" because its size belies the vast resources it marshals in hot pursuit of an idea or innovation.

Not long ago a visitor inquired, only half facetiously, whether the iceberg reference was appropriate in light of its association with the ill-fated *Titanic*. A Chrysler executive replied, "Well, the iceberg survived." What has enabled Chrysler itself not merely to survive but to flourish is the company's ability to tap resources throughout its "extended enterprise"— a term that Chrysler, in a flash of next-generation foresight, trademarked several years ago.

Shareholders applaud the benefits achieved through Chrysler's resource management, as indicated by Figure 5–1, which contrasts Chrysler with the industry average for the years 1992–1999.

DEFINING NEXT-GENERATION INNOVATION RESOURCES

Next-generation innovation resources are not simply expenses on an income statement or projections in next year's budget. Nor are they only the

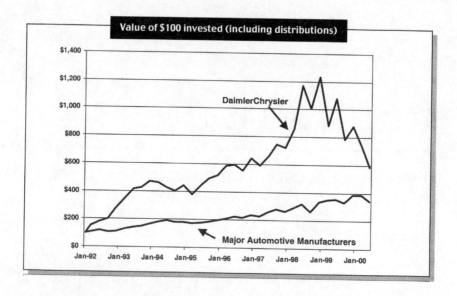

FIGURE 5.1   Chrysler shareholder returns vs. industry average, 1992–2000
Source: Tradeline®/Dow Jones Interactive, Arthur D. Little Analysis.
NOTE: DaimlerChrysler stock has been indexed to Chrysler stock which ceased trading on October 23, 1998 following Chrysler's merger with Daimler-Benz.

facilities—the laboratories, the office space, and the equipment—that people use in the process of innovation.

Resources also include financial support, of course, as well as employees, suppliers, partners, customers, even competitors. Add to these the knowledge, the competences, and the technology within an enterprise, and you begin to get an idea of just how extensive next-generation innovation can be. The challenge and the opportunity is to manage the company's intangible assets with the same drive and discipline that it manages tangible assets.

Next-Generation Resources Are Suppliers

It is no wonder that more than three hundred potential suppliers line up to do business with Sun Microsystems. Based in Palo Alto, California, the computer giant directs over $4 billion a year to a handful of suppliers led by Sony, Seagate, Solectron, Samsung, and Zytec. And for Sun it's money well spent: the company has managed to cut its own costs dramatically

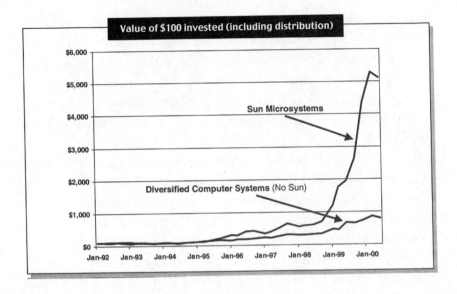

FIGURE 5.2 Sun Microsystems shareholder returns vs. industry average, 1992–2000
Source: Media General Financial Services.

while streamlining product development and perfecting design and delivery so that the right component arrives in record time.

Sun's success stories continue to multiply.

Item: Research-and-development personnel at Sun invited engineers from Zytec, Seagate, and Solectron to participate in the design and development of new computer boards as well as a host of other products for networks and servers. This teamwork has helped cut product development time in half, and Sun can now roll out new products in less than a year.

Item: The Sony Corporation has built a factory of its own near San Diego, California, where it manufactures monitors for Sun's computer systems. Proximity has helped inspire a coordinated effort between supplier and customer, both sides working as a single team to reduce lead time from four months to barely more than two weeks.

Item: Sun sells its computer products in some 170 countries, but this widespread distribution has increased the problem of meeting demand. Alphanumeric keyboards are needed with symbols in a host of languages, because the most popular languages—English, French, Japanese, and German—simply do not meet all customers' needs. To prevent inventories from piling up, a Sun supplier came up with the clever innovation of building keyboards with blank keycaps. As orders are received, the supplier stamps the blank keys with the appropriate symbols, thereby satisfying demand in record time without creating a costly storage problem of unsold keyboards.

At Chrysler, just as at Sun, managing and innovating across the supply chain does not mean issuing edicts from the top. Rather, there is a dialogue, a symbiotic collaboration inspired by mutual rewards and underlined by a recognition that survival may well depend on just how well the two sides cooperate on projects and programs essential to both.

Who pays the cost of a project? The percentage that Chrysler bears is a matter for friendly but firm negotiation with suppliers. On major projects, it tends to be 50–50, but exceptions are numerous. Tom Moore, head of Chrysler's Advanced Technology unit, recalls that eighty-five suppliers joined with Chrysler engineers to develop and build an electric car, with the suppliers paying 50 percent of the costs. More than five hundred people who technically were not employees of Chrysler took part in this joint effort.

On one concept car, Moore continues, the brake manufacturer fully funded the brake work, while Chrysler funded all the systems related to the vehicle's suspension. Project costs for the seats were equally shared, whereas the exterior trim was divided 60–40, with Chrysler bearing the larger share.

The rights to innovations developed with suppliers generally depend upon the funding arrangement. If Chrysler pays all innovation costs, it retains the right to use an invention for its own applications—though the supplier-partner is not restricted from using it for other applications. If the supplier company has borne the costs, it holds the rights, but Chrysler is free to use the invention.

Such arrangements are not uncommon in other settings. At a university, for example, scientists might use the laboratories, research tools, libraries, intellectual property, and other resources in performing their investigations, then share the fruits of their discoveries with the institutions at which the research was carried out.

At Chrysler, project managers bring in two or three key suppliers at the beginning and employ them until the project's conclusion. So long as they don't "drop the ball," as Moore puts it, so long as a new invention appears that they can't match, those suppliers know they're in for the long haul—perhaps five or ten years.

They also know that they will need to focus all of their attention on the one project, whereas one of their competitors may well be working next door on another project. The decision as to which supplier gets which assignment is made by Chrysler's technicians and project managers, who rely on the supplier's recent performance, not on personal relationships with buddies at one or another vendor company. All arrangements are cleared with the proper authorizing departments, including purchasing.

For Chrysler, the management of its supplier resources has led to a secondary task: teaching suppliers how to manage their vendors. The importance of this task is anything but secondary, however. "We get messed up by the dumbest things four levels below," Moore says. A fuel gauge once used on the Jeep Grand Cherokee, for instance, showed there was still gasoline in the car even though the fuel tanks were actually empty. It turned out that Chrysler was buying a preassembled component that included the fuel tank, pump, and sending unit. The problem was in the sending unit, which tells the fuel gauge how much fuel is left in the tank.

To correct the problem, a Chrysler team started with the first-tier supplier, who sent them to the maker of the sending unit, who in turn sent them to the company that produced the electronic parts of the unit. From there the team found its way to the company that made the printed circuit board. Once confronted with the problem, representatives at this fourth-tier supplier company made the following acknowledgment (in not so many words): "Now that you mention it, our ink supplier did make a change in his formula, but we didn't think it would make any difference."

Of course, it did make a difference. The differently formulated metallic ink used in drawing the circuits was not as durable as the previous ink, and it wore out rapidly. The defect disabled the circuit board and, ultimately, the electronics and the fuel gauge. The company making the ink had no idea that its product would be used in the construction of a car.

In the end, the Grand Cherokee's fuel gauge worked fine, but the experience taught Chrysler managers to be ever vigilant for problems that can arise at any level in the complex web of suppliers and vendors. Chrysler, in effect, had to manage an even larger extended enterprise, teaching its first-tier suppliers to communicate down through each successive tier the importance of keeping a constant eye on the work of every vendor.

How has this cooperation with suppliers paid off for Chrysler? The story of the automaker's recovery from bankruptcy is practically legendary, and although no one would go so far as to attribute its rebirth solely to constructive relationships with a few cooperative suppliers, those relationships are nonetheless part of Chrysler's self-prescribed remedy for curing its ills.

Next-Generation Innovation Resources Are Partners

Next-generation companies demonstrate a willingness to work with others as equals in the relentless search for the innovation premium. That means sharing information and expertise rather than holding fast to private or proprietary knowledge. It also means learning how to treat partners with respect and to work with them to develop projects that are truly mutually beneficial.

Sun Microsystems has a knack for enlisting the support of its many partners. Since 1996, for instance, Novell, Inc., and Sun have teamed up to combine networking software and Java technology, thereby enabling customers to create applications for their Internet or Intranet sites. As an added benefit, this partnership between Novell and Sun's business unit, JavaSoft, is helping drive the creation of other technologies such as voice-recognition software and speech synthesis.

Fast approaching next-generation status, Sun Microsystems does not allow innovation to be confined within its own four walls or to be constrained by an internal R&D budget. Rather, innovation extends forward and backward along the value chain to include suppliers, partners, employees, and customers.

Next-Generation Innovation Resources Are
People and Their Competencies

Often, organizations are trapped in traditional views of the roles people can play: scientists work in labs; machinists work at lathes; accountants work at computers. All make their contributions in their assigned areas, and that's the end of it.

There is another layer, as it were, of worker contributions achieved by the teams we call networks. These networks comprise employees who, in addition to their everyday assignments, are permanently on call to help in the pursuit of special innovation projects—those that require their special expertise. Chapter 6 will investigate these teams more thoroughly, but for the moment consider the work of technology clubs at Chrysler.

The leveraging of Chrysler's people through the technology clubs has its counterpart in the higher echelons of the company, where those on the vice-presidential level are given oversight responsibilities for areas far removed from their normal duties. The purchasing vice president, for example, might be told to watch over the large-car platform, or the manufacturing vice president might oversee production of the minivan.

In addition to the benefits of an extra oversight, this two-hat arrangement makes for more interconnections. Thus, dependencies develop within the top ranks, which in turn support the company's goal of teamwork and cross-fertilization. "There's almost nothing in the company that an individual or even an individual function can do unilaterally," says Tom Moore. "It's all very much a team process."

Next-Generation Innovation Resources Are
Assets That Must Be Systematically Managed

All next-generation resources lie fallow until they receive the investment that will turn them into actions. The degree and seriousness of commitment by everyone in a company's extended enterprise will distinguish a next-generation performance from that of an also-ran.

Lucent Technologies, Inc., based in Murray Hill, New Jersey, creates telephone and other communications systems and software as well as microelectronic components. It showed 1997 revenues of $26 billion. In conjunction with its Bell Laboratories unit, Lucent receives, on average, three new patents each business day, a number attributable in part to the 24,000 bright and inspired researchers who work at Bell Labs. The rate of innovation remains an object of envy for other companies, which only dream of meeting the Lucent's benchmark in innovation.

Leveraging both its financial and employee assets, Lucent devotes approximately 12 percent of its yearly revenues to research and development. In 1998, it established Lucent Venture Partners, Inc., a $100 million venture-capital fund that hunts down and invests in small companies working on emerging technologies in areas of interest to the parent company. Lucent thus benefits by way of information and profits from advances it considers too costly, too risky, or too time-consuming to pursue in-house.

Another next-generation pathfinder, Cisco Systems, has invested heavily in small firms in the high-tech industry. Since 1993, it has put close to $7 billion of venture capital into companies that are almost certain to become some of its best customers for Internet switches and routers. Cisco isn't necessarily aiming to use venture capital as a shortcut to an ultimate takeover or acquisition of a small firm. In many cases the company hopes merely to gain access to the smaller firm's innovation and technology. With investments in companies such as CLASS Data Systems in Israel, Cisco has extended its enterprise around the globe and locked in a diversification strategy that will propel it well into the next century.

ARE YOU READY FOR NEXT-GENERATION INNOVATION RESOURCE MANAGEMENT?

Change Your Mindset

Part of the secret of leveraging resources is mental attitude. You must learn to think beyond your traditional boundaries, outside functional silos. No longer limited to the resources of a research-and-development organization, you can and must look to all the people, equipment, and other resources that exist in the skein of allies and partners that make up the company's value chain.

They are not necessarily owned by your company, however, so you cannot automatically assume they will be immediately available. But the chances are that you will be able to borrow or share or tap into these deposits of knowledge and experience if you play your cards right. Tom Moore explains how it works at Chrysler: "Before we even know what we want or how to do it, we put together a team of suppliers, and then we invent it together."

When Chrysler embarked on its co-innovation policy with suppliers, the company's competitors shook their heads, insisting that those outsiders could not be trusted. The arguments bandied about have been reiterated in many a tradition-minded company: work with outsiders on an invention and the first thing you know, they'll sell it to the competition. You'll lose all your secrets.

That mindset, once common at Chrysler and still operative at scores of other companies around the world, presents a formidable barrier. There is always some risk that one will lose secrets, but, in general, Moore believes that the benefits are well worth the risk. "The only leaks we at Chrysler have had are from employees who quit," he says. The gain has far exceeded the risk, as suppliers and partners add their experience and competencies to the innovation process.

"Let's say Johnson Controls (one of the companies that makes seats for Chrysler) is going to provide prototypes for the next concept," Moore offers as an example. "We don't just say, 'Okay, we want a seat shaped like this and weighing this much.' We don't just give them mere specifications. Rather, we bring them in, give them office space to work in, and explain the philosophy of the entire vehicle. We want them to see how the seats have to be coordinated with the interior design, the floor plan, the vehicle's structure and safety features, the instrument panel, and the customer's total vehicle experience." With a deeper understanding of the project, the supplier can better work to create parts that help achieve the overall vehicle goals.

For all the partnering, Chrysler remains in control of the product. "Let's say we want a new seat that has a manual adjustment function. We don't let JCI talk us into an expensive power seat. We control the package and the content of the features and the weight and the cost margins," Moore adds. The project is a continuous design process in which the supplier completes its assignment in constant consultation with the customer, adjusting to whatever changes become necessary as the project evolves.

We believe this tier-by-tier analysis and communication must become standard operating procedure for a next-generation enterprise. The key is to take nothing for granted. Next-generation managers cannot afford to assume that every supplier and vendor down the line has every bit of needed information; they must be willing to ferret out vendors at every level and make sure that no one is in the dark about what products are needed and how they are to be used.

In addition to sharing essential information about product development and uses, next-generation R&D managers have to be willing to listen to suppliers' suggestions for developing innovative products and services. Five hundred people from various suppliers brought in to work on an electric car at Chrysler represent a force of tremendous intellectual power, one that must not be hamstrung by preconceived notions. The key is to allow flexibility within acceptable and manageable limits, to align rather than overmanage suppliers with projects.

See Where You Stand

Here is a quick questionnaire to help you understand where you stand regarding next-generation resources:

- When you consider your company's resources, do you think of them as expenses?
- Can you name your intangible assets? Or, when you think of resources, do you picture simply property, equipment, and cash on hand?
- Do you see your employees as an expensive, albeit necessary, asset?
- Does pouring revenue back into research and development feel like pouring money into a black hole?
- Can you accurately account for the core competences that form the basis of your company's success?
- Do your employees know their worth? More importantly, are they assured that you know their worth?

- How wide is your resource net? In other words, when you fish for available resources, do you cast outside your company territory?
- What amount of risk is your company prepared to take? To what extent will you rely on the resources of partners or collaborators? To what extent will you share your own resources with them?
- How eager are your suppliers to work with you instead of your competitors?
- To what lengths do you go to share product ideas with your suppliers? At what point in a product's life cycle do you bring in their experts?
- How often do you arrange meetings with your partners to share knowledge, experience, and ideas?
- How trusting are you of those suppliers and partners who contribute greatly to your success?
- When was the last time you listened to—and pursued—an idea proffered by an external source?

Don't be surprised if your answers to these questions are not flattering. Most managers find that they—and therefore their companies—are not particularly enlightened when it comes to how they value their innovation resources and intangible assets. They tend to focus on tangible assets, such as retail outlets, manufacturing plants, machinery, and monetary investments, and try to ignore the intangibles, such as employees' knowledge, intellectual property, and external partnerships. Most managers realize that although they are eager to seek out innovation, they are reluctant to put their financial resources into projects that don't have immediate visible and measurable returns.

As we have seen, Chrysler's relationship with its suppliers is unique and extremely progressive. And even though the benefits may be obvious, most managers are threatened by the notion of sharing project plans with external suppliers or partners. Not only do they find it difficult to view their own employees' knowledge as a valuable asset, they overlook the potential value to be gained by sharing in the intellectual property of external groups. For the sake of secrecy and control, most managers miss out on the enormous benefits offered by exchanging knowledge, testing ideas, and sharing experience.

FOLLOW THE PATHWAY TO NEXT-GENERATION INNOVATION RESOURCES

Resist the Temptation to See Resources in Purely Budgetary Terms

Yes, the budget committee does provide a major resource, but if you consider only the financial aspect, you may be overlooking the value that your suppliers, partners, customers, and employees can add to the innovation premium. If organizations like R&D, engineering, and technical services are treated as cost centers, they will behave like cost centers. If they are treated as investment vehicles to drive innovation and growth they will respond accordingly.

Leverage What You've Got

Resources will always be limited, so look for ways to leverage what you've got to what you can accept. Assess your innovation assets—your people, partners, stockholders, customers, facilities, and finances. Often a supplier can help you innovate and improve performance—or vice versa—but you have to be open to the possibility. That will require a change of attitude about "control" and what you consider to be proprietary.

Eliminate Barriers

Be willing to break down walls or at least create passages to allow your suppliers, partners, and customers to access important and relevant information and resources you hold or control. This works both ways, of course: You will need information and insights about products, processes, and potential uses for new inventions that may be held by your suppliers and partners.

Use Your Innovation Platforms and Partners to Make Investments in Human Resources and Competencies

To turn a phrase from President Clinton's 1992 campaign—it's the people, stupid. No matter how comprehensive your innovation strategy and process are, it all comes down to execution. You need to develop world-class competencies in the areas that are most critical to your growth and you need to put the best people in the best place to bring innovation to life. To do this, you have to develop human resource investment plans that reflect the clear differences between the objectives and strategic value of the various platforms and networks discussed in Chapter 3. The most significant investments should be aligned with Level I and Level II platforms (*Business, Performance and Growth, and Innovation and Development*). These platforms are accountable for developing and exploiting business innovations as well as accelerating the transfer of knowledge and learning. Leaders of these platforms are accountable for building the company's excellence in a given area, managing the human resource investments in the area, and capturing value from it for the company. Investments in Level III platforms (*Excellence and Leadership Building*) are more focused on building world-class excellence through internal and external networks, while Level IV platforms (*Knowledge and Learning*) require more investments in infrastructure and networking to leverage existing competencies.

Get the Most From Your Intellectual Property

Intellectual property assets and patent portfolios are getting more and more attention these days. Investors and managers are seeing a shift away from conventional asset management and a shift toward knowledge-intensive aspects of the business. Transfers of intellectual assets, even among foreign subsidiaries, are increasingly subject to taxation. And financial managers are compelled to develop balanced score cards that more explicitly take intellectual property into account. For companies like 3M who have always managed intellectual property as a corporate asset, the challenge is how to invest and manage these assets across the extended enterprise to increase the value they can yield. For other companies the challenge is in finding ways to exploit the value of these assets across their markets and business units. As a first step in meeting that challenge, you have to develop an understanding of the relative value of your intellectual property, bundled in a variety of ways. Only then can you target which areas to invest in for the future. With this understanding and strategic direction you can develop explicit asset management plans around these bundles of intellectual property including patents, trade secrets, knowledge, etceteras.

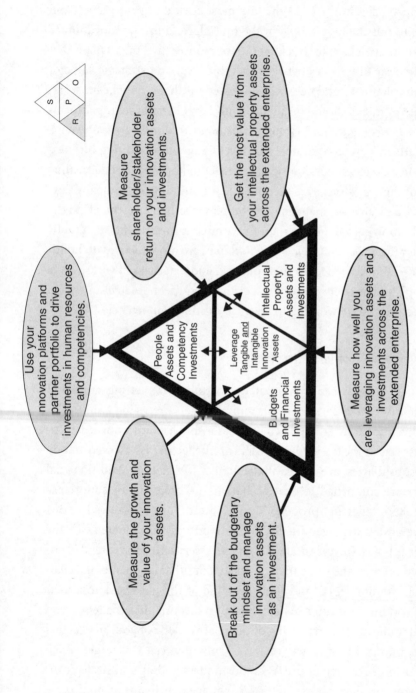

Next-generation companies leverage tangible and intangible innovation assets to accelerate the pace of innovation.

FIGURE 5.3 Moving down the pathway to the next-generation innovation resources
Source: Arthur D. Little, Inc.

Develop Innovation, Resource, and Asset Management Plans

Develop resource-management plans for all your assets—tangible and intangible. You can and should be actively managing intangibles like customer loyalty, brand, supplier preference, partners, and employee retention/attraction, along with the more tangible resources of property, plant, and equipment. Although such plans offer considerable flexibility, they still demand that resources be *explicitly* valued, that you have policies and programs in place to maintain or build these resources (or write them off), and that you have clear metrics in place for evaluating and tracking investments in these assets.

Businesses today evaluate most investments with a straight return-on-investment measure. This is the most easily understood tool to use in managing the bulk of R&D investments. When you invest in innovations, however, it is clear that you can't fully depend on this old standby since it doesn't really address the major issues: commercial and technical risk management; multiple benefits ranging from accelerated cost reduction (easy to measure) to shareholder value; and the various innovation premiums.

Think about combining the quantitative elements from traditional valuation methods, such as cash flow and risk analysis, with systematic qualitative assessments from the technical, commercial, and legal perspectives. It's part hard-core analysis and part calculated guessing, but the premise is that you can isolate the contributions different resources make to your business. Once they are isolated, they can be economically quantified.

VARY THE PACE

••

Create Worldwide
Networks of Innovators

Twenty miles outside of Pittsburgh, Pennsylvania, stands a world-renowned research-and-development center. The Alcoa Technical Center, with a staff of 700 and a budget of $100 million, is home to numerous innovations—the first lead-free machining alloy, for example. Created by Alcoa in 1997, the alloy gave manufacturers a strong yet environmentally friendly material that, unlike conventional lead-bearing aluminum alloys, improves machinability.

Although originally known as the Aluminum Company of America, the onrush of globalization challenged any notion that Alcoa could remain isolated in the United States. In the automotive industry, the largest potential market for aluminum, for instance, GM's and Ford's move to global purchasing and product development helped push Alcoa to internationalize its own operations.

In fact, more and more of Alcoa's markets—from beverage cans to airplanes—were similarly affected by rapid globalization. With major customers like the Coca-Cola Company betting the bank on growth abroad, Alcoa knew it couldn't afford to restrict itself to a single geographical area. The European consortium, Airbus Industrie, for example, became a real player in a market long dominated by Boeing.

Worldwide expansions and cross-border integration meant that Alcoa's innovation management had to reach into all corners of its vast global operations. Innovation could no longer be isolated and restricted to the center near Pittsburgh. In 1997 Alcoa's leaders and senior managers, including the chief technology officer, Frank Lederman, decided that the company needed a global network of innovators—not necessarily restricted to Alcoa employees—working together and sharing information about their discoveries. In other words, Alcoa had to restructure its organization according to next-generation principles.

Alcoa's Frank Lederman recruited Dr. Greg Smith from outside the company as the director of central technology capabilities and charged him with helping to drive this worldwide corporate initiative. It was clear to Smith that, to provide effective support, the technical center had to be fully integrated with both the corporate business units and the manufacturing plants. As Smith puts it, the goal was "to move beyond mere downsizing and continuous improvement projects and to create a much more powerful innovation and technology engine."

To that end, new teams were created to ensure that the organization works as smoothly as possible. The Alcoa Technology Board is the forum where senior leaders set direction and emphasize critical issues such as aligning innovation strategy with corporate vision, determining high-level goals, and approving the strategies and operating plans of the various business units.

The business units' operating plans are developed by Technology Management Review Boards (TMRB). Several TMRBs, comprising both business and technology leaders, were formed around clusters of business units to drive cross-unit initiatives and investments within areas such as smelting, refining, chemicals, extrusion, and milled products. The boards also set strategy, lead technology deployment, and drive innovation and ideation within their business units.

In addition to these process-oriented boards, some manufacturing TMRBs help drive product technology advancements in aerospace and automotive markets, and they are being considered for such areas as construction and packaging. As Alain Belda, Alcoa's chief executive officer, sees it, "We need more involvement of the business units in the management of resource-unit functions. We need more pull and engagement."

"The key to the TMRBs' success," according to Greg Smith, "was to start from the top and quickly engage the boards in strategic decisions that needed to be taken. Once the first few TMRBs had set their strategies and goals, the other parts of the company saw the value and followed suit. The next step was to make the strategies operational and real. We used the strategies to determine where the gaps were and how best to close them through transfer of best practices and existing technology or through innovation and development."

Then came the establishment of a wide range of both formal and informal innovation networks and platform teams. At Alcoa, a platform is a cluster of technologies and competences with a significant impact on business results. Smith says that "this understanding of 'we know how to'—meaning that we have the technology and competency—resides throughout the company, in people and knowledge management systems at R&D, in engineering centers, in development factories, in the plants themselves, or even outside the company with a valued partner."

In addition to focusing on seamless collaboration across the extended enterprise, Alcoa embarked on an aggressive campaign to lower costs and increase the return to shareholders through continuous improvement and the introduction of the Alcoa Production System (APS). This system emphasizes elimination of inventory and other wastes, make-to-use production, highly reliable and efficient manufacturing techniques, and automation. It's a system that could not operate in a traditional organizational structure characterized by divisional interests, turf wars, and proprietary knowledge.

The results of Alcoa's stream of product, process, and organizational innovations are reflected in many ways, not the least of which is its return to shareholders. As Figure 6–1 indicates, the company's shareholder returns between 1992 and 1999 confirm Wall Street's favorable view of Alcoa's leadership and commitment to innovation.

Looking beyond the aluminum platform, Alcoa has used its innovative ways to succeed well outside its traditional realm. For example, Closure Systems International (CSI), an Alcoa subsidiary that originally manufactured bottle caps and other metal closures, acquired H-C Industries, Inc., in 1986. H-C owned a patented compression molding process to make closures out of plastics. Alcoa incorporated the H-C technology to devise plastic bottle caps that alert a consumer to tampering, and then went on

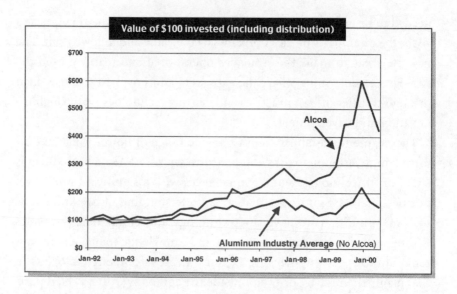

FIGURE 6.1 Alcoa shareholder returns vs. industry average, 1992–2000
Source: Media General Financial Services.

to become the world's leading supplier of tamper-proof closure systems to the soft-drink market.

Although new ideas and discoveries still largely come from a core group of Alcoa employees, the company now defines its organization in a way that looks far beyond its corporate walls. All members of Alcoa's extended enterprise—customers, suppliers, partners, allies—can be and are invited to join the innovation effort. Customers such as Boeing and Coca-Cola, who had pressured Alcoa to innovate with them, have become as much a part of Alcoa as Alcoa is a part of their extended enterprises. Whether it is reducing costs in a customer's manufacturing processes or helping create new concepts and products, Alcoa is ready with the full battery of its own innovations.

DEFINING NEXT-GENERATION INNOVATION

Next-Generation Innovation Organization Is Fluid

Ideas flow effortlessly from one part of the enterprise to another—between senior leaders, managers, employees, customers, partners, and suppliers—without having to pass through a complicated system of checks and balances. Even if the enterprise extends over a wide geographical area and encompasses different cultures, languages, and information systems, innovative ideas move quickly and smoothly across boundaries to those who need them and can put them to productive use. In a next-generation company you won't hear, "Sorry, we can't read this file," or "That's a great idea but try convincing the finance department to support it."

Next-Generation Innovation Organization Is Leadership: From the Top Down and the Bottom Up

The role of innovation management leaders is critical to the success of the enterprise.

This role extends far beyond the management of either centralized or decentralized R&D operations. A chief development officer (CDO) is responsible for managing the innovation process from the top down, from concept to customer, and for creating and capturing value in both the technology and product-process development pipelines. He or she must also seek to maximize the return on innovation investments and to leverage key innovation resources inside and outside the company.

Successful leaders of innovation management are not simply technology-minded autocrats. Nor are they purely makers of business deals. They are, in a sense, like coaches of all-star football teams. They are not out on the field scoring touchdowns, but they are creating the conditions that make it possible for the entire organization to lead the league.

The CDO's mandate is to inspire and motivate team players to get out there and win. Like the great coach, the CDO informs, instructs, and encourages from the sidelines. These senior innovation leaders inspire the hearts, minds, capabilities, and powers of other key players, whether leaders are new employees or external partners.

Innovation-driven SAP AG, a company that enlarged its overall staff by more than 40 percent in 1997, exemplifies this method of leadership. The company places a high priority on coaching programs that educate newcomers and promote an environment of creativity and initiative. Teamwork informs an organizational structure that tolerates mistakes but emphasizes entrepreneurial responsibility for results. Dr. Hermann Kager-

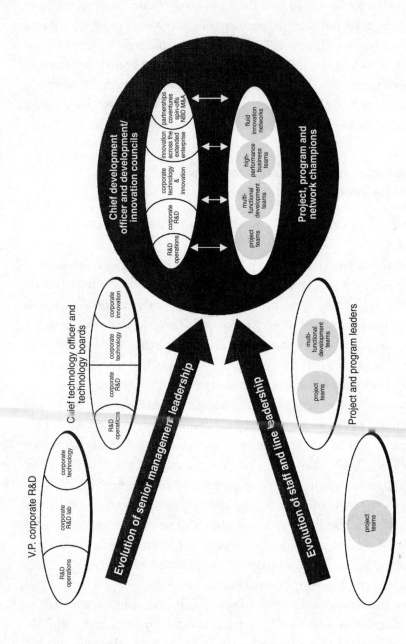

FIGURE 6.2 Next-generation innovation is about leadership
Source: Arthur D. Little, Inc.

mann, chief executive officer of SAP, says the coaching program at SAP is an essential source of innovation within the company: "We each consider SAP our baby, so we care a lot about what our younger colleagues make of it."

It is imperative that the next-generation CDO not be left to go it alone in this endeavor. If innovation is to be sustained, a new culture of inquisitiveness and a hunger for new ideas must be encouraged and supported throughout the company. All senior managers must set the charge, get involved, and manage innovation collectively in boards and councils. At Alcoa the CTO, Frank Lederman, believes that the only way to improve R&D effectiveness and increase the speed at which innovation and technology are deployed throughout the organization "is to engage the business leaders in the management of technology and innovation."

SC Johnson, the Racine, Wisconsin, maker of chemical products for the home, takes a similar view to organizational reporting lines, eliminating barriers between innovation and its implementation. William D. Perez, the company's president and chief executive officer, has a straightforward message for the company: "We need to be 'product plus' in all of the products we deliver to our customers." By that he means that customers should prefer the SC Johnson product over that of competitors in blind label testing. His philosophy is that only in this way will innovative and high-quality products continue to build brand image and equity. This is a far cry from the old GE approach of merely sourcing and branding consumer electronic products, betting on the strength of the brand rather than the sustainable, innovative performance of the company.

Strong senior leadership for innovation also is in evidence at the Eveready Battery Company's Energizer unit. As Pat Mulcahy, chairman and chief executive officer, explains, "We have set up an Innovation Council that has senior managers from technology, marketing, and business unit management. These will be the people who will set the course for innovation, not based on hunches or convictions but on knowledge and intelligence from the market, consumers, and the competition. If you see how our innovation process works, you will see what our future will look like. We will be a different company."

Joe McClanathan, the company's former CTO and now its vice chairman, emphasized the message when he told Energizer employees, "Product innovation is not a project. It has no beginning and no end. It is a culture, an attitude, a basic and pervasive desire to improve the way we improve our products." Energizer's Innovation Council reports to Mc-Clanathan, as do the competitor-intelligence, sourcing, and partnering functions, which help to extend the reach for innovation beyond the company itself. In addition, McClanathan's presence on the executive committee facilitates the removal of barriers against innovation and ensures that the innovation mindset is anchored at the top of the company.

Next-Generation Organizations Are Networked

Senior leadership can initiate and inspire, but innovation networks serve as the arms and legs, the eyes and ears, to do the actual work of the next-generation organization.

Networks, which are based on mutual appreciation of capabilities and contributions, do not replace the existing organizational structure and processes. They require a lot of informal communication through casual meetings, e-mails, exchange of think pieces, and the like, and they also need a "node," an initiator and stimulator who, from time to time, draws conclusions and suggests new directions. This role develops through acceptance and fellowship, not status and authority.

Networks involve people from different hierarchical levels and use different communications systems. They are clearly accountable, but they are not programmed. They arise out of a common interest or theme that holds people together and that makes it desirable to be part of and actively contribute to them. Leaders of these networks, which typically reach across boundaries, are recognized as having enterprisewide roles, development objectives, and accountabilities.

Companies can stimulate networks by encouraging informal communication and by recognizing and supporting the network builders. Networks also usually involve outsiders, contributors from the professional community, suppliers, customers, even academics. Members may variously be highly active and challenging, creative, permanent, or temporary.

Networks can be categorized into three types:

1. *Intelligence and monitoring networks* are concerned with the future and pay attention to customers, end users, markets, the industry, technologies, and the shop floor. They generate new ideas or concept fragments and maintain relationships both within the company and across the extended enterprise.

2. *Excellence and capability-building networks* establish and maintain leadership on key innovation platforms and actively manage and support them. These networks are accountable for the following: excellence in their platform across the extended enterprise; rapid deployment and transfer of innovation and appropriate enabling technology; active monitoring of projects and initiatives at plants, suppliers, and partners; and building and managing the company's tangible and intangible assets in the platforms.

3. *Innovation and development networks* are accountable for creating high-value and high-impact results. They are supported by well-coordinated investments and by well-connected individual project teams, as well as by internal and external capabilities. They are accountable for creating and managing the technology and product-process development pipelines; capturing the value of new products and processes; creating awareness within management of the platforms' strength, weakness, opportunities, and threats; and pushing the platform's envelope with respect to its technologies and capabilities. In addition , they should have a say in deployment of resources and actively build capabilities, actively coordinate and leverage investments, synthesize project-program and internal-external trade-offs, and propose them to senior management.

At Chrysler, networks are called technology clubs, a name that confuses outsiders (Tom Moore says his competitors think they're social clubs). In reality, they are teams of highly motivated people who are knowledgeable about a particular automotive system—for example, the chassis, the steering, or the radio system—or a particular cluster of technologies, such as speech recognition or alternative fuels. Their mission is all business: they seek to build virtual resources around their club's system and create strong business value as their innovations are incorporated in one or another manufacturing process or in a particular model's platform.

The technology clubs serve as a conduit for sharing information among various parts of the company. Tom Moore's Advanced Technology unit, for example, reviews the status of its projects with the appropriate technology clubs, seeking their ideas and advice. In the past, Moore says, his unit would simply have gone its own way and shared completed projects with other technical people in the company. Now the unit benefits from technology-club wisdom all through the innovation process while also passing along its own discoveries to benefit other parts of the organization.

The information-sharing function of the clubs extends to key suppliers and partners outside the company, too. Chrysler seeks intelligence about new technologies and innovations beyond its gates by maintaining close connections with university research operations. Like many companies in industries ranging from pharmaceuticals to aviation and space exploration, Chrysler knows that investment of resources in research centers at universities can pay off in both new products and new minds, especially when it comes to recruiting for the company.

Chrysler's technology clubs are dedicated to building capabilities and leadership in their particular areas, seeing to it that the steering or chassis mechanism, for instance, is constantly improved through the sharing of information and best practices. At Chrysler teams responsible for product development and technology development really do know "what Chrysler knows." They bring to the table the knowledge, experience, and intellectual capital of the extended enterprise. Club members feel collectively responsible for the company's commitment to excellence, and they are held accountable by management. Their salaries reflect their success.

Next-Generation Innovation Organizations Have Partners

Next-generation innovation organizations depend on nurturing partnerships both externally, with nonpartisan groups as well as competitors, and internally, between departments. These partnerships must be worth maintaining from both sides' point of view. A recent study reported in the *Harvard Business Review* indicated that more than two-thirds actually fail to fulfill the expectations of both partners. Failure can be avoided if business leaders seek out partners less for their similarity in product or service offering and more for the best practices they exhibit, the technical competences they possess, or the real technologies they have developed.

We saw an example of the necessary foresight at Robert Bosch GmbH, the leading manufacturer of electrical and electronic car systems. Although not widely known among the general public, Bosch has been a hidden giant among automotive suppliers for decades. Bosch has gained a reputation for pioneering work by ingenious and loyal employees. As the globalization of markets and technologies continues apace, the company is capitalizing on this renown and expanding a sophisticated set of partnerships, often moving outside the customary confines of the automotive industry.

One such partnership is being cultivated with Deutsche Telekom, the former German telecommunications monopoly, and Debis, the IT division of Daimler-Benz (now DaimlerChrysler). Working in the advanced field of electronic car navigational systems, the group is jointly developing a product called DYNAPS, a combination car-radio, mobile-telephone, and navigation system. Linked to a public traffic-message channel, this computer-based system receives information from terminals measuring traffic flow and volume along highways and major roads. It then generates navigational instructions for the driver, allowing someone in congested areas to choose an alternative route.

Industry experts are expecting that electronic car navigational systems such as DYNAPS will generate a worldwide market volume of several billion dollars annually by the year 2010.

The business of automotive subsystem development is costly but potentially highly profitable. Thus, while Bosch pumps a sizable percentage of revenues back into research and development, its main focus is on ferreting out breakthrough opportunities through other collaborative arrangements around the world.

For instance, in the area of antilock braking systems (ABS), in which Bosch is considered a pioneer, it has entered into a partnership with Nabco Ltd., Jidosha Kiki Co., and Nippon ABS Ltd., all of

Japan. (Bosch already holds 50 percent of the capital of Nippon ABS.) For steering systems, it has formed a joint venture with ZF, a leader in the area of gear and transmission systems. With a major change from hydraulic to electro-hydraulic and electrical steering systems on the horizon, ZF and Bosch are combining their know-how to gain advantage.

External partnerships and collaborations like these will keep Bosch at the forefront of innovation.

Next-Generation Innovation Organizations
Reach Across and Beyond Boundaries

Two decades ago Peter Nicholas and John Abele met on the sidelines of a soccer field in Boston, Massachusetts, as they watched their children at play. Nicholas was a businessman and Abele a researcher. It wasn't long before they discovered a promising compatibility of skills and interests, and so was born Boston Scientific.

Founded in 1979, the company was dedicated to the manufacture of innovative medical devices for the health-care industry. It has since moved from the sidelines to a starring role. In fact, Boston Scientific is now a $1.5 billion organization that leads the field in forecasting, influencing, and fostering technological advances in the health-care industry.

To be sure, there have been pitfalls along the way. In 1988, for example, the company showed a loss of $900,000 on sales of nearly $100 million. But only five years later, its earnings approached $70 million on sales of $380 million. Boston Scientific has continued to grow mightily, both in revenues and market share, helped by a series of canny acquisitions.

The real key to the company's recent success, however, has been the redesign of its organizational structure along next-generation lines. The prime mover in that regard is Art Rosenthal, who in 1994 was named chief technology officer.

When Rosenthal assumed the post, the company's research-and-development department was closely aligned to central headquarters and tightly controlled by marketing. "The research-and-development group was largely made up of manufacturing people who did development as a sideline," Rosenthal explains. "There was no outreach from the people in research and development to the medical users of the devices they were making. Marketing acted as an interceptor."

Rosenthal convinced management to decentralize Boston Scientific's research-and-development function. Specialized technology managers and their staffs were assigned to appropriate business units, closer to the customer and to the exchange of new technologies in their particular specialties. Technologies that were used across the board were maintained in a central research-and-development core.

When companies were acquired, they were mined for new technologies. Rosenthal cites the purchase of SCIMED Life Systems, Inc. in 1995: "Other people saw SCIMED as simply cardiology," he says. "We saw it as a technology platform that we could leverage for other businesses."

To keep the flow of ideas and new technologies circulating throughout the business, Rosenthal set up what he calls a "technology executive council," which meets for two full days every six weeks. Each member brings the perspective of his or her division to the group's debate over how much to allocate to various projects. In these council meetings participants have the opportunity to share knowledge gained from their own experiences and to keep colleagues informed about technology platforms and core activities.

The goal is, at first look, a paradoxical one: to maintain strong central oversight while posting the divisional research-and-development units nearer the front lines and giving them greater operational freedom. As Rosenthal describes them, however, these divisional units are his arms, legs, eyes, and ears. "They are the link between the academic community, the technological breakthroughs, and the end users of the product," he says. "It's somewhat organized chaos, but it works extremely well."

ARE YOU READY FOR NEXT-GENERATION INNOVATION ORGANIZATION?
Change Your Mindset

Organizational behavior and development is a tough nut to crack, but, as always, a change in mindset is the starting point. Most organizations are built up over years and years of both bad and good behavior, and are permeated with assumptions and attitudes that develop from the mix of strong personalities and company policies toward work and its rewards. To transform any organization into one supportive of next-generation innovation, you must encourage collaboration and reward risk-taking. It is an attitude that must be as evident in the bottom administrative sphere as it is in top management policies.

What, for example, does company literature say about the organization? Does it reflect a company moving forward or one that is rooted in rules, traditions, limits, and boundaries? Do policy manuals endorse "thinking out of the box," or do they stress the need to toe the line and observe traditional rules?

Furthermore, are you inspiring your sales force with innovation vision only to rein them in with cost-cutting measures? Are you asking for leading-edge ideas from your research-and-development division but then clamping down on the scope of its initiative the minute a project fails? What standards do performance measures enforce?

The signals you send, both in your writings and your actions and values, reflect the message you are conveying about innovation. If you expect your employees to embrace innovation, you must practice what you preach.

See Where You Stand

How do you begin building a next-generation organization? Ask yourself the following questions:

- How often do you get all your business unit managers together in the same place to share knowledge and exchange different perspectives?
- Are your key research and development people on the front lines or in the back room?
- Does your marketing department intercept the transfer of ideas between company researchers and customers?

- Is innovation merely a word in your company or an underlying culture?
- Are your senior managers inspired to innovate but unable to transmit that message to employees?
- Have employees sensed the urgent need for innovation but still face the resistance of budget-bound executives?
- Do innovative ideas frequently get held up between conception and commercialization by complicated rules at different stages? Do they end up in black holes?
- Do you have specific people in place to eliminate possible barriers, whether internal or external, between innovation and its implementation?
- Is your passion for innovation matched by your partners and collaborators, or are you expending too much effort trying to inspire them?
- Is your company active in pursuing its strategic vision of the future, or merely reactive in responding to the work of competitors?
- Are you out in front of your organization attempting to score goals on your own, or are you leading the entire team to victory?
- Do you ask for evidence of innovation from your staff, only to then rein them in, cut off their departmental budgets, or punish them for failure?
- Does your company constitute its own insular world, or do you have a team of "scouts" constantly investigating the surrounding business terrain?
- Are your business teams comprised of the key people critical to the success of innovation?
- Is your technology leader kept out of sourcing and procurement decisions, or is he or she given the necessary authority to help propel innovation forward?

Despite the push toward a more horizontal organizational structure during the last decade or so, many managers will still find this review dif-

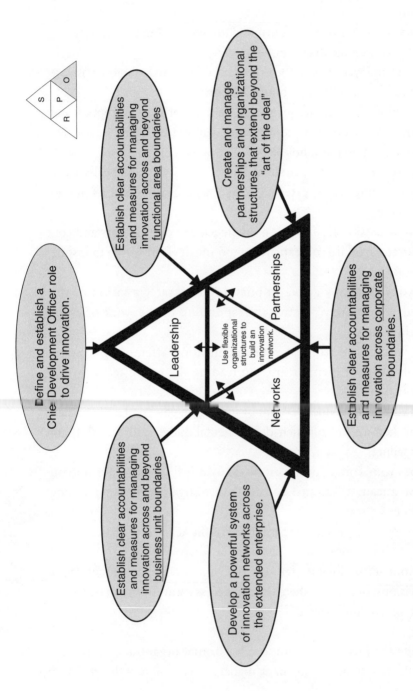

Next-generation companies use flexible organizational structures to build powerful innovation networks.

FIGURE 6.3 Business innovation from the top down and the bottom up

Source: Arthur D. Little, Inc.

ficult. They undoubtedly will discover that they head up less of a networked organization and more of a group of disparate units, all with the same goal, perhaps, but each with its own methods for reaching that goal. In such organizations innovative ideas do not flow smoothly from the idea stage through development to rollout. Instead, they are blocked—by different processes used at different stages, by lack of communication, or by varying levels of commitment to innovation.

Many managers find that, although ideal in theory, establishing networks is difficult in practice. Employees may be protective of what they know and may be reluctant to share their knowledge with other departments, much less external partners. Or they may be eager to participate but stifled by the shortsighted vision of middle managers who have not fully bought in to the message of innovation. Even more disturbing, many managers may discover that they themselves are the real impediment to a well-networked organization.

FOLLOW THE PATHWAY TO
NEXT-GENERATION INNOVATION ORGANIZATION

Build Enterprise-wide Leadership for Innovation

Many companies already have a shared vision of business innovation at their executive-committee level. Where this is true, it should serve to drive a consistent message of innovation across the business and its key functions.

However, as with many new initiatives, there is the critical issue of sustainable leadership. Will the executive committee have the energy to stay focused on this initiative? Or will they go back to their "day jobs"? Can they even get close to the level of commitment reported by Sony executives, who say they spend 80 percent of their time on innovation? If so, the executive committee should continue to own the innovation initiative. If not, there will be a definitive need to augment the executive committee's key role with complementary roles for one or more boards or councils that can be actively devoted to innovation and development.

Define and Establish a Chief Development Officer Role

Even with strong collective senior leadership for innovation, there is invariably a need for a single point of accountability for managing such a networked organization. Before the CDO can have any hope of injecting fluidity across the organization, they must answer the following basic questions:

- What kind of power or influence do you need to be effective?
- Who will be your arms and legs, eyes, and ears?
- What kind of resources will have to be created or mobilized?
- Are your company's goals and objectives and performance measures well aligned with those of your partners across the enterprise?
- Do you have sufficient influence in procurement decisions and in mergers and acquisitions?
- If not, how will you manage coventuring or sourcing?

Answers to these important questions will differ, of course, but in every situation the attitude and position of the chief development officer (or chief innovation officer or chief technology officer—the title is less important than the leadership the person provides) will determine the climate for the entire organization. Thus, it is vital that the CDO's behavior and the company culture it helps generate reflect the desired outlook.

Determine What Kinds of Innovation Networks You Will Need, and Manage Them Explicitly

Managers must first figure out what kind of innovation networks they need and then populate them with the right people. Each player is accountable to contribute a critical capability so that the network as a whole, reflects the company's overall insight and experience.

Supporting such networks on a continuing basis requires a good communications infrastructure within the organization, as well as collaborative discussions among business and functional leaders, all of whom are closely involved in the day-to-day work of their own teams.

Create and Manage Partnerships That Outlast the "Deal"

Volumes have been written about the disappointments and failures attributed to a wide range of organizational structures for managing joint ventures, strategic alliances, and other partnership arrangements. Very often the lesson learned in the aftermath is that exhaustive effort goes into the deal, the specific transaction, and the details of product/technology transfer, but little thought is given to the development of a portfolio of innovation initiatives or a true innovation engine that will sustain the partnership. Accountabilities are unclear, loyalties split, and metrics unaligned. Leading innovators focus substantively on aligning organizational structures for the partnership, and on managing the broad range of details and links necessary to create growth and innovation for all parties.

Use Flexible Organizational Structures to Build a Stronger Network

Different business units may be at different stages of innovation, so networks and partnerships should be set up in such a way that they enjoy the highest leverage and cause the least disruption. A successful pilot network is sometimes a compelling force to gain acceptance for other networks across the organization.

Alcoa uses different structures for different networks. For example, the smelting function's Like Technology Teams (LTTs) are first organized around the primary technology used and are then divided by region if appropriate. In essence, the person who is in charge of technology at a site is the highest-ranking member of the network. When deemed necessary, an ad hoc team can be instituted to look into and solve a specific subprocess problem or conduct a specific due-diligence assignment. It can also function as a permanent team to create and implement long-term performance enhancement program for the subprocess.

Jerry Roddy, director of technology for Alcoa's primary-metals division worldwide, says that using the LTTs allows "the people in the different plants to know who to call when they have a problem. But LTTs are also extremely effective in rolling out an innovative technology worldwide," Roddy says.

"An added advantage," he continues, "is that at every acquisition Alcoa makes anywhere in the world, we have a 'natural home' for the acquired units. We can immediately start the postacquisition integration work and transfer technology and best practices from us to them and vice versa."

John Sibly, Roddy's counterpart at Alcoa's refining operations worldwide, notes that key to making "these technology transfers work is to have good audit protocols that can be used by the networks. You need to be able to quickly figure out where we are now and what gaps to work on."

"Once the gaps are determined," adds Greg Smith, "the platforms and networks can start working on closing them. It is then that the real innovation starts, using brainstorming sessions or computer-enhanced ideation."

Elsewhere in the company, Alcoa managers have organized networks around a process step, as in the case of aluminum ingot, which Alcoa produces for its own use or to be sold. "The ingot network at Alcoa is one of the mature networks and operates very well," says Smith. "It has good leadership and has created metrics that allow the sharing of best practices across the company and that emphasize where and how to focus our innovation efforts."

Establish Clear Accountability for Management of External Alliances and Partnerships

Next-generation companies need to shift their focus beyond just top-down and bottom-up organizational structures to horizontal structures that will support collaboration across the extended enterprise. Since these relationships are clearly critical to innovation leadership, they need much more attention than they have been given them to date. In particular, they can't be structured by procurement officers or lawyers who don't share the company's perspective on the need to create partnerships to drive innovation.

Deemphasize Functions

Companies aspiring to next-generation status are likely to find traditional organizational ladders and boundaries obsolete, constraining, and ineffective. In the drive to capture the innovation premium, companies will depend more and more on cross-functional teams and networks that drive bottom-up innovation and on a wide range of groups that look to business or market pull for ideas.

Linking these together will be a host of activities that can be leveraged to draw up the results curve and to create at least a threshold momentum for sustained innovation. Indeed, the notion of "functions" may gradually disappear altogether, at least for purposes of generating ideas and pursuing the most innovative ones to fruition.

SUSTAIN THE PACE

• •

Build a Culture of
Continual Change and Learning

The British Petroleum Company (BP) is a sleek, focused money-making machine. Indeed, it is one of the most profitable of all the major oil companies, capable of embarking on aggressive acquisitions campaigns and significantly outpacing the industry in shareholder returns between 1992 and 2000 (see Figure 7–1). Less than a decade ago, however, the picture was anything but rosy. Back then, BP was a debt-ridden, confusing conglomeration of divisions involved in different fields.

How was an industry behemoth transformed into a lithe, flexible, and innovative organization? By making learning an innate component of the corporate culture, says John Browne, BP's group chief executive and managing director since 1995. "Learning is at the heart of a company's ability to adapt to a rapidly changing environment," Browne declares. "It is the key to being able both to identify opportunities that others might not see and to exploit those opportunities rapidly and fully."

When Browne took over his current leadership role in July 1995, British Petroleum was trying to fight its way back to financial health after a devastating decade that saw company debt reach an all-time high of $16 billion by the end of 1992. And record debt was only the most visible of the problems then plaguing the company: reserves were shrinking, BP fields in the North Sea and Alaska's North Slope were beginning to dry up, and

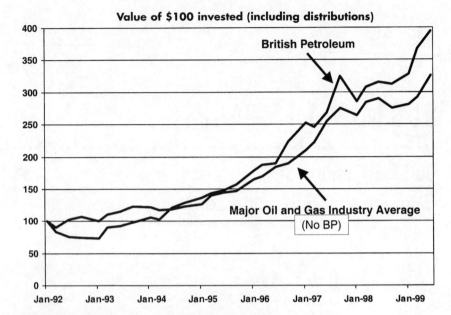

FIGURE 7.1 British Petroleum shareholder returns vs. industry average, 1992–1999
Source: Tradeline®/Dow Jones Interactive, Arthur D. Little Analysis.
Note: Stock prices and dividends for non-U.S. companies have been converted from their local currency to U.S. dollars for this comparison.

the company's exploration-and-development costs were at least three times higher than those of its competitors.

Today, however, debt is down by almost 60 percent, BP has established a strong presence in new regions like the Middle East and South America, it has an annual output growth rate of more than 5 percent, and it has been able to embark on a series of major acquisitions. As BP managers see it, much of the credit for this transformation and the creation of a strong innovation-and-growth engine must go to their commitment to consistent, companywide learning.

Becoming an organization adept at gleaning, sharing, and using knowledge is high on the list of priorities for BP managers. "The top management team must stimulate the organization, not control it," Browne contends. "Its role is to provide strategic directives, to encourage learning, and to make sure there are mechanisms for transferring the lessons."

Central to BP's learning mechanism are its performance-improvement teams (PITs). At BP every employee must recognize his or her personal responsibility for the performance of the entire enterprise, and the PITs help them to do that by putting in place growth and performance measures that stretch across divisions, business units, and even enterprise boundaries.

Instilling a sense of enterprisewide responsibility is particularly important at a company like BP, which is divided into business units grouped according to activities or assets. The great advantage of an asset-based organization, according to BP management, is that it puts tremendous emphasis on performance delivery within a particular asset enterprise. The risk, however, is that people might become so internally focused that they would lose sight of what's happening outside their own endeavors. The PITs help to eliminate this risk and create a more balanced focus on the management of knowledge-based and intangible assets.

Not surprisingly, information technology plays an important role in forming BP's learning communities and also in maintaining a sense of overall purpose by facilitating a rich exchange of knowledge and experience within the flexible framework of asset groupings. In fact, the technology center is deliberately referred to in BP parlance as a "shared petrotechnical resource" to emphasize that those who work there are working for more than one asset most of the time.

Another method of encouraging knowledge sharing and enterprisewide learning is BP's peer-assist program (this tool is also used to reinforce the notion of teamwork). Instead of bringing in an expert to determine what should be done when problems arise, employees are encouraged to seek out solutions themselves within the shared learning environment. And by using the computer-based network to explore avenues of assistance, a person with a problem can range as far afield as necessary to find the needed expertise.

Next-generation companies like BP recognize that until acquired knowledge is combined with other knowledge and then made available to workers in a clear and usable form, it is inert and cannot generate the real driver of innovation: ideas. Thus, knowledge, competence, and technology networks are used to ferret out and advance knowledge and information from a decentralized universe of intelligence. In this way the entire organization can survey the grand sum of its intellectual capital and, by combining data in new ways, effectively leverage existing knowledge to produce still more.

In the next-generation environment a fluid, networked organizational structure stands ready to redeploy these newly minted ideas and best practices back across the extended enterprise.

Since knowledge management and learning are continual, the company keeps getting smarter and smarter. And that makes it possible to constantly improve the product and service-development process, thereby lifting the organization's long-term market value.

DEFINING NEXT-GENERATION INNOVATION LEARNING

Next-Generation Learning Is Central and All-Encompassing

If a little learning is a dangerous thing, as poets warn, innovation-led, next-generation companies sidestep that danger by making learning anything but little. Instead, learning is all-encompassing, with a company's energies focused on promoting constant and accelerated learning in every corner of the business and across the broad reach of the extended enterprise.

Overlaid onto the areas of strategy, process, resources, and organization, learning becomes the crucial fifth pathway that winds itself around the other pathways, holding them together to produce the next-generation innovation business model. It is the learning environment that enables an organization to capture the set of *sustainable* benefits that define the innovation premium. By definition sustainability requires a steady flow of new ideas and insights and effective pathways to commercialization and rollout. But encouraging quantity does not mean forsaking quality. The stream of ideas must be bounded first by the establishment of good criteria as to what is being sought, and second by the use of an efficient mechanism to sort and channel what is found.

In sum, intelligent strategy is combined with innovative process and creative use of resources, which are then supported by an efficient and flexible organizational structure. The flow of ideas thus harnessed promotes yet another requirement for sustainability, a mastery of the knowledge being acquired.

Next-Generation Innovation Learning Is
Distributed Across the Enterprise

Building distributed enterprisewide networks is a key element in the transfer of knowledge. Next-generation companies use knowledge, competence, and technology networks to unearth and develop ideas from all manner of decentralized satellite repositories.

Throughout British Petroleum's recent stages of recovery and growth, company managers relied heavily on the ability of enterprisewide networks to foster cohesiveness. "You can change the structure, break it down into business units, and change reporting lines, but the thing that will hold an enterprise together is its networks," says David Jenkins, the company's former chief technology officer. "They are an essential piece of the fabric of the enterprise."

As BP well knows, following its recent merger with Amoco, learning networks also allow next-generation companies to accomplish integration of merger-and-acquisition partners without the disruption, dissension, and outright chaos that typically accompany such moves.

When one company acquires another, it naturally wants to integrate the newcomer into the culture and organization as quickly as possible. In the past, that typically meant bringing key people to headquarters and showing them the ropes, or dispatching a SWAT team to do the same job at the acquiree's headquarters. But neither approach is effective. Why? Because they are top-down and thus reflexively resisted.

Integration by inclusion is the goal of a next-generation company. The acquired company is immediately connected to the enterprisewide learning network, through which its workers can absorb the new technologies, processes, and culture as members of a peer group, not as subordinates. The pride and confidence of the new workers are reinforced, and their alignment with the objectives of the combined organization proceeds smoothly and rapidly.

In commenting on the many ways that an enterprisewide learning network can be put to use, BP's John Browne enthusiastically observes, "You can learn from your own experience. You can learn from your contractors, suppliers, partners, and customers. And you can learn from companies totally outside your business. All are crucial."

Hilti AG, the Liechtenstein-based producer of fastening and demolition systems for the construction industry, is a master at learning from its customers. Recognizing that the people who use its products are those best suited to offer constructive criticism, Hilti asked twelve experienced installers of industrial pipe to evaluate its assembly of fasteners and supports used to hold pipes to walls and ceilings. As a result, Hilti was able to make significant, commercially useful improvements in its pipe- support product in about half the time—and at half the cost—required by a traditional product-development route.

Hilti's approach to learning is a model of next-generation principles. Concentrating on both product *and* process innovation, the company gathers ideas from every corner of its extended enterprise while maintaining a firm commitment to finding out firsthand what its customers really want.

ARE YOU READY FOR NEXT-GENERATION LEARNING?

Change Your Mindset

When we use the term *learning*, we are not talking simply about information management or knowledge networks. What most concerns us is the way next-generation learning transcends the bounds of continual improvement to stretch an organization's leaders, workers, partners, suppliers, customers, and even competitors to build insights and grasp *sustainable* innovation.

Sustainable innovation is not a static position that you aspire to and eventually reach. Nor can you guarantee your company the fruits of the innovation premium by confining next-generation techniques to only one of the five pathways. Instead, innovation is a dynamic state attained only when the entire company learns how to learn and how to keep on learning. Therefore, the next-generation enterprise must be a perpetual learning machine.

A company that desires to reap the profits of competitive advantage and build shareholder confidence must ensure sustainable growth and value creation. And achieving those twin objectives rests on the company's ability to constantly improve its knowledge-gathering and sharing process, its technology and innovation platforms, and its core capabilities. These elements, in turn, can grow and thrive only in an environment that prizes knowledge and ideas as prime resources, and manages and deploys them efficiently throughout the extended enterprise. In short, an organization must create a climate of learning that exists not for the sake of learning, but also for the sake of innovation.

See Where You Stand

How do you promote next-generation learning? Begin by asking yourself the following questions:

- Do you encourage only your top key people to learn or is learning a company-inclusive activity?
- Have you made it a priority to install one person whose sole responsibility is to champion more effective learning within your company?
- Have you picked your learning leader because he or she is just like you? Or do you recognize that it may take a different type of leader to inspire innovation, one who can also teach the executive committee how to become innovative?
- Is every person in your organization, both internal and external, involved in continual learning?
- When looking for new ideas and product feedback, do you turn to your customers last?
- When spreading the innovation gospel, do you fall into the trap of convincing your employees that the "old way" is now worthless?
- Have you forced innovation on your company? Or are you trying to instill it from the inside out?
- Does every employee feel the urgency of the need for innovation and the validity of his or her own individual contribution?
- Is the knowledge in your company possessed by individuals or by networks? In other words, if someone in your company leaves, does what they know walk out the door with them?
- Does your company think of a "team" as a group of disparate individuals thrown together to work on a one-off project?
- Do you stress interaction and knowledge sharing between your company's different business areas?
- Is your information technology department considered a separate entity? Or is it a vital learning link for all departments alike?
- Are all the leaders at your company constantly on the go? Is reflection time considered "down time" and therefore wasted time?

- When was the last time you scheduled a meeting to reflect on lessons learned rather than merely planning the route forward?
- From whom do you request constructive feedback—from your suppliers, contractors, partners, and customers, or merely from "experts" outside your normal business sphere?

Conducting a learning review will be an eye-opener for many managers. Most companies today are notoriously bad at gathering, disseminating, and using knowledge. Learning is not emphasized as the all-encompassing, company-wide responsibility it needs to be. Instead, it is often relegated to the job of only one person—or at best, one department.

Although it is a good thing to make one person responsible for building a company's ability to learn, many managers assume the job is then finished. They lose sight of the fact that until learning has become a top priority for every member of the organization, even the most innovative company will become merely a knowledge and information sieve with a cumbersome and outdated reservoir of data.

Determining how their company rates on its approach to learning forces managers to recognize two things: learning requires both time for reflection and assessment, and a willingness to receive—and, indeed, seek out constructive criticism.

Even if company leaders are willing to expand learning programs, most are unwilling to take the necessary time to reflect on lessons learned. They forge ever onward, convinced that their time is *always* best spent on forward-looking projects. Furthermore, while they may be willing to bring in external experts to help them assess company results, they rarely seek out the opinions of those who matter most—the company's own suppliers, partners, and customers.

FOLLOW THE PATHWAY TO NEXT-GENERATION LEARNING

Make Sure Your Innovation Leadership Is Also Providing Learning leadership

Accelerated and constant learning must be championed by whomever is leading the quest for innovation—whether a chief technology officer, a chief development officer, or some other senior leader. This leader must be an educator from the outset, teaching budget-bound senior management that technology and innovation are not simply overhead expenses but rather generators of potential profit centers worthy of investment.

After executive backing has been secured, he or she must carry the message to the entire organization, enlisting workers' approval and eager participation in the challenge to achieve innovation and maximum value. But the leader must also recognize that the workers, having grown up with a different model of how to create value, are unlikely to embrace a new one overnight. They will come to expend cooperative effort only as they understand and accept next-generation principles and goals. The savvy leader will assure workers that their current expertise will not be superseded but enhanced and rechanneled, and that innovation will be stimulated, not compelled.

Reinforce the Notion of Organization-wide Teaching and Learning

Although leaders are responsible for managing organizational learning so that employees are effectively aligned in value-creating business units, no one person is solely responsible for cultivating innovation by encouraging learning. A greater emphasis on learning must be spread throughout the entire organization—it is every leader's job.

Establish "Natural" Standing Teams to Foster Sustainable Learning

Natural standing teams dedicated to progressive innovation and development help to ensure the sustainability of innovative learning at next-generation companies. In current business models, teams are given a mandate, a goal, and some money and then are sent off to get the job done. When they complete that task, they go back to their normal work. In that sense, the growth they achieve is not sustainable. The next-generation organization, on the other hand, realizes that long-term success requires more than ad hoc teams and one-shot projects. So it establishes natural standing teams whose learning curve is not a steep, task-specific incline followed by a drop-off, but rather a steady, cumulative, and sustainable rise.

Networked systems give support to the team's leadership and provide a steady stream of knowledge with which to continually expand workers' expertise, broaden team competences, and augment best practices. Under the traditional approach, experts became team-capability leaders but there was little continuing effort to build higher levels of expertise. If an expert were lost, projects were often seriously delayed as the organization scrambled to develop a replacement. Next-generation learning balances that risk and assures that more individuals are able to bring the knowledge and experience of the extended enterprise to their project teams.

Set Aside Time to Reflect on Lessons Learned

Time for reflection is crucial for the sustained learning demanded by next-generation innovation. Unlike previous business generations, next-generation companies such as BP recognize that dialogue and reflection are vital if, as one BP manager puts it, "you want to actually learn from what you do."

A competitor, Shell Oil Company, would raise no objection to that statement. Believing that "tomorrow's most successful corporations will be those with the greatest capacity to learn," Shell has set up an entire complex devoted to learning in a setting specifically designed to be conducive to discussion and reflection.

Using traveling faculty, outside experts, and "technology designed for long-distance learning," Shell plans to launch programs intended to enlarge its capacity for innovation and help employees deal productively with change and ambiguity. By embracing new ways of thinking, responding to challenges, and leveraging talent and resources, Shell believes that it can "create more win-win situations within Shell and with customers and suppliers."

WIN THE RACE

••

Capture the Innovation Premium

Innovation is one of the prime forces behind the longest-running expansion in the history of the North American economy. The growth conferred by innovation in strategy and customer management, in operational performance, in product, process, and service creation—all underpinned by a strong entrepreneurial culture and improving information technology—shows signs of smoothing out the highs and lows, if not actually repealing the traditional notion of business cycles.

That innovation should spew out benefits on such a grand scale would, no doubt, gratify even Joseph Schumpeter. You will recall that the late Harvard economist, whose work we cited in Chapter 1, defined innovation not in terms of a single product or service, but as the entire creative process—from the first glimmerings of an idea right through each stage of development until the marketable good or service is delivered to the customer. Schumpeter believed that true innovation is powerful enough to change the economy.

We agree, and we think that the remarkable growth we have witnessed in recent decades gives credence to Schumpeter's theory. But more important, as an increasing number of companies come to understand this power, and as they adopt the next-generation principles we have outlined in these pages, the potential for steady, long-term, sustainable economic growth seems to be limited only by our collective imagination.

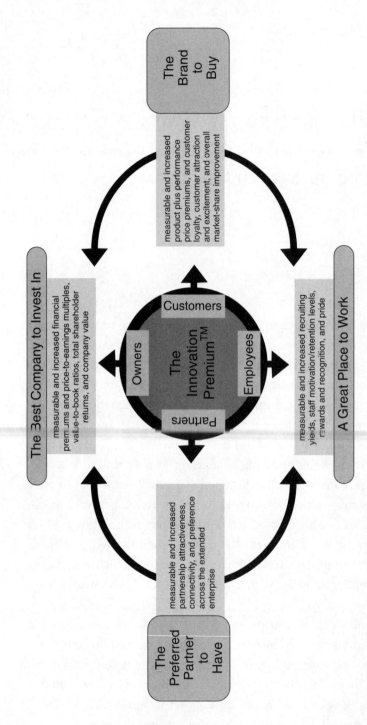

Business Innovation creates and captures high value premiums across all the company's stakeholders, including shareholders, customers, employees, and partners.

FIGURE 8.1 The four dimensions of the innovation premium
Source: Arthur D. Little, Inc.

In preceding chapters we've visited a number of companies in a wide range of industries that are driving high-performance innovation along and across the five pathways of strategy, process, resources, organization, and learning, propelling themselves into the next generation of innovation leadership. Now, in this final chapter, we turn our attention to what capturing the innovation premium specifically means for customers, employees, partners, and shareholders.

CAPTURE THE INNOVATION PREMIUM FOR CUSTOMERS

Next-generation enterprises typically recognize that their creativity benefits customers by providing valuable new products and services and high levels of customer satisfaction—the *raison d'être* of any business. And they stretch to excel even further by focusing on specific customers and treating them in innovative ways. They go the extra mile to make it easier and more worthwhile—even exciting—for their customers to do business with them.

At Canon, for instance, the strategic decision to create unique systems rather than the typical copy-cat electronic products means that the wants and needs of individual customers take on added significance. Direct customer input is an increasingly valuable resource that is actively sought and leveraged to facilitate both product and process innovation. Lead customers become part of Canon's extended enterprise, which further increases the benefits they enjoy from this innovation engine.

At one level, what Canon is doing, of course, is simply targeting a certain segment of customers, tailoring its offerings to the group's buying needs and preferences, and then soliciting customer feedback to continue the process in an ever more efficient and productive manner. But soliciting feedback to facilitate customization of products isn't the only way in which companies innovate and customers benefit—far from it. Next-generation companies are also coming up with differentiation strategies to help pinpoint *why* a given customer would buy from them. That, in turn, allows the companies to leverage their strengths in inventive ways and offer customers a clearly articulated and compelling value proposition.

Furthermore, these companies are seeking to increase two-way communication with customers. Using a mix of traditional methods (sales calls and call centers) and newly emerging options (the Internet, electronic kiosks, and electronic commerce), companies are giving customers more ways in which to make their opinions known.

One of the most promising paths to customer innovation is a change in the way leading companies look at business processes: by moving to the other side of the counter to sample the view from the customers' perspective, these innovators are helping to ensure that each process delivers customer experiences that will engender long-lasting loyalty.

Finally, companies are capturing the innovation premium for their customers by leveraging information technology. Acutely aware of the key role information plays in sustaining competitive advantage, innovators are willing to invest in the sophisticated technology and database systems that will allow them to build customer relationships and support strategic decision making. This growing desire on the part of innovators to do whatever it takes to build productive relationships can only increase the benefits accruing to customers.

Regardless of the technique being used, we have found that, at a minimum, innovation in *any* form translates into greater customer satisfaction and a favorable image for the innovative company in the marketplace. Beyond this, sustainable innovation leadership often translates into customer excitement and loyalty, brand equity, superior price premiums and margins, and dominant market share.

The effects, then, are both tangible and measurable in a company's customer metrics. They help a company to secure current customers and acquire new ones who will add still more value through increased purchase volume, a lower cost to serve, and word-of-mouth referrals.

A good example of multidimensional customer innovation is Cisco Systems, the global leader in networking for the Internet. Dubbed "the corporation of the future" by *Business Week*, Cisco uses cutting-edge technology to build the powerful networks that link businesses to their customers and suppliers. In addition, innovation is very much apparent in the realm of customer intimacy: remarkably, Cisco's leading customers routinely provide input into the strategic planning process, because the company believes that customers know more about what Cisco needs than do top executives.

Cisco is perceived as the leading networking company for hardware, software, and service. It also has the most recognized name in networking equipment. Rising rates of customer satisfaction (85 percent of customers describe themselves as satisfied) are a firm indication that Cisco's customers are well aware of the benefits they receive from this industry leader's innovative ways—benefits that ultimately accrue to its shareholder as well.

CAPTURE THE INNOVATION PREMIUM FOR EMPLOYEES

Leading-edge companies have leading-edge employees. The best and the brightest are drawn to forward-thinking, innovative companies because these companies create extraordinary value for their employees. They treat employees as individuals, integrating personal needs and interests with the needs of the business, and they strive to offer meaningful rewards and recognition—using the resources accumulated from successful innovation.

The best and the brightest like the risk taking as well as reward sharing that goes along with innovation. They like holding exciting jobs in dynamic organizations in which they have high levels of responsibility and a variety of tasks and assignments. They like a continuous learning environment and a supportive atmosphere that encourages creativity without fear of punishment if new ideas don't always pan out.

In much the same way that the exchange of benefits between customers and innovative companies fuels a self-perpetuating cycle, so, too, with the employee relationship. Innovative companies attract the best employees, who turn in the best performance, which attracts still more of the best employees, who further fuel the engine of innovation.

Unlike traditional companies, which are bogged down in an operating model focused on systems and on maximizing the return on physical, financial assets, next-generation companies recognize that competitive advantage built on technologies or systems alone can quickly erode. They know that people are the only asset that appreciates with use, so that, in the long run, companies compete on the basis of people, not technology.

In other words, innovative companies have recognized knowledgeable workers as assets whose recruitment, motivation, development, and retention is essential to long-term success.

As Herb Kelleher, the chief executive officer of Southwest Airlines, a company widely known for its family-like atmosphere, puts it, "Amazing things happen when you make people feel they are valued as individuals, when you dignify their suggestions and their ideas, when you show your respect for them by allowing them to exercise their own wisdom and judgment and discretion." Southwest successfully leverages its human capital assets in its pursuit of continuous innovation.

Innovative companies find ways to lift the performance of their employees well beyond the norm by freeing the initiative, creativity, and drive so long stifled by the traditional environment. They do it by putting in place programs to develop individual capabilities and collective competences—programs that far exceed threshold human resource department requirements—and then making sure that these mechanisms achieve what they are designed to achieve. As a result, employees view the company as a valuable means of attaining their personal and professional goals.

Continuous learning is vital to a next-generation company, of course. In a function that can best be described as "company as university," leading companies offer continuous learning for employees who strive to enhance their sense of self-worth and improve their business performance. Learning may take the form of classroom training, on-the-job coaching, or extrapolation from day-to-day experiences.

Continuous learning, in turn, feeds the company's commitment to regularly renew activities and deploy people in exciting new capacities. And regular renewal is essential for an employee to sustain high performance. In today's continually evolving business environment, both a company and its employees can often find themselves in situations where rapid change is demanded. It is essential to support affected employees during any change and to use the change as an opportunity for growth.

Another distinguishing feature of a next-generation company is the way it develops its employees' ability to carry out informed and balanced risk taking. Employees are buttressed by a supportive environment in which

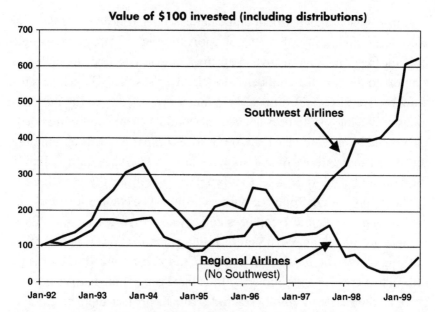

FIGURE 8.2   Southwest Airlines shareholder returns vs. industry average, 1992–1999
Source: Media General Financial Services.

there is no penalty for daring to color outside the lines—even when the finished product ends up in the wastebasket.

"If you want to have an innovative enterprise, you need people to be comfortable with taking risks," says Atul Arya, group planning manager at British Petroleum. "You're never going to really move forward on innovative technology unless you're comfortable with taking the risk that's associated with it and understanding the nature of the risk. . . . The very important thing is not to go looking for someone to shoot [when things don't work out as intended]. It's a greater question of recognizing that [the company] took a whole series of risks at a very senior level in terms of the way the project would go forward. And people were trying to deliver.

"It's very interesting," Arya continues, "to see [what happens] in an enterprise when something goes wrong. It's like captains of ships. Does the top of the tree recognize that, in actual fact, it's their fault, and not blame the people down in the enterprise? Old style is to look for somebody to blame."

John F. Welch, Jr., chairman and chief executive officer of the General Electric Company, says that "the object is to build a place where people have the freedom to be creative." Still, most individuals need guidance and support to develop the confidence to take the risks that will help a company grow and remain innovative. Whereas the traditional managerial focus on business systems deadened the confidence and ability that people needed in order to take risks, innovative companies focus on building up those traits and teaching employees how to take the smart risks, informed and balanced gambles that produce a payoff for the company.

The supportive environment typical of innovative companies motivates creative employees and recognizes and rewards their learning, achievements, and risk taking. What's more, leading organizations make sure that nothing blocks the flow of information and communication that is so critical to a creative environment. At the same time, though, they are sensitive to the needs of employees and strive to protect their health and safety.

In sum, the innovation premium that next-generation companies create for their employees produces a highly motivated workforce with a low turnover rate; it also attracts still more of the best talent on the job market. The end result is that a talented and inspired bunch of high-performing people improve the business at a much faster rate than competitors can manage. It should come as no surprise that the most innovative companies across industries are also those that are also typically ranked as the best places to work.

CAPTURE THE INNOVATION PREMIUM FOR PARTNERS

Partnering is vital to next-generation enterprises. In the face of shrinking product-development cycles, rising development costs, rapid technology changes, and increasing customer sophistication, innovative companies recognize that they can't go it alone. So they build extended networks of partners, sources, and suppliers to capture emerging opportunities by acquiring and leveraging competences, both internal and external, and by accelerating technology transfer and the pace of commercialization.

Forming exciting and profitable new channels for product creation, distribution, process-development, and rollout allows next-generation companies to speed the development and time-to-market of winning products, helping to ensure future earnings growth and value creation.

In other words, partnering and the extended network are essential to the value equation that enables leading companies to command the innovation premium—and thus capture value for those very same partners. Yet again, we encounter the same self-renewing circle of value creation found in both the customer and employee relationships.

Where do innovative companies partner? We believe that the success of innovative companies hinges on the quality and longevity of their collaborative relationships. Success hinges on two key factors: knowing where and when to partner, and executing fair and equitable agreements that lay out specific outcomes and reasonable yardsticks of performance.

Strategic alignment is an important consideration, of course, and alliances are usually sought to fill competence gaps and accelerate time-to-market. But unlike most companies, which tend to partner with suppliers in technology ventures and sourcing activities, innovative companies differentiate themselves by partnering up and down the value chain—not just with suppliers, but with customers, competitors, and other industry participants. By stepping outside the usual bounds of collaboration, innovative companies derive value from accelerated commercialization as well as from technology venturing and sourcing.

Next-generation companies also tend to license out ideas that fail to meet the internal hurdle rate, thereby creating an extended and loyal network of sources and partners. In some high-risk partnering arrangements, the innovative company might choose to absorb near- and medium-term operating costs in order to give a venture the time and resources needed to produce sustainable results for the partners over the long term.

Among the innovative companies we have visited in previous chapters, some are further along than others in their pursuit of the innovation premium, but all are committed to collaboration. Exemplifying this commitment is Millennium Pharmaceuticals. Although partnering relationships are standard operating procedure across the pharmaceuticals industry, in both market access and technology development, Millennium's clever use of collaboration fairly screams next generation. The biotech company rocketed from a start-up to break-even level for three of its first six years, largely due to its partnering strategy.

In work scarcely dreamed of two decades ago, and which casual observers still might find akin to science fiction, Millennium is combining cutting-edge technology with cutting-edge science to find ways of delivering disease-fighting drugs to specific genetic targets. And it is making profitable use of partnering at every step of the way, having raised more than $1 billion dollars from its partners.

Readily admitting that it is garnering top dollar, Millennium attributes its financing success to its status as a "premium player," able to deliver the innovative technology its partners are seeking. And since partnerships and alliances are two-sided affairs, with benefits ideally accruing in equal measure to each, Millennium's remarkable string of collaborations suggest that it is, indeed, delivering uncommon value to those companies with which it chooses to partner.

Top-tier innovators such as Millennium, Chrysler, Sun Microsystems, and others highlighted in these pages provide extraordinary value and benefits to suppliers, partners, and other collaborators as a measurable consequence of successfully implementing programs to build the extended enterprise. Many companies, of course, claim to have highly productive external networks and partners, but the most innovative ones create value and improve earnings performance across the extended enterprise. They develop and exploit opportunities within the network but do not view these relationships from a pure win-lose or a contractual perspective. Rather, innovative companies build a sense of trust and create excitement levels that make them extremely attractive to investors, customers, employees, suppliers, and partners who desire to become part of a winning organization in a relationship that creates value.

CAPTURE THE INNOVATION PREMIUM FOR SHAREHOLDERS

Traditionally, financial markets have assigned value to companies using a variety of quantitative and qualitative measures such as revenue and earnings, both historical and anticipated. The change in a company's market capitalization versus that of its competitors is a yardstick for determining industry dominance and success. So, too, is an increase in market share. But the question that most concerns us is: What part of shareholder value does innovation drive? Does an innovation premium exist? All else being equal, does the market accord greater value to the more innovative company's equity? We are convinced that it does.

Witness Nokia. By changing its focus to wireless-communications-based technology and innovation platforms, and by paying close attention to customers desires, the once little-known Finnish company has become the premier player in its field, surpassing the giant Motorola in worldwide mobile-phone sales. The name Nokia has become synonymous with innovation as the company outlegs its competitors in the race to provide so-called smart phones.

A revamped product-development process, together with strong support systems across the extended enterprise, closer relationships with suppliers, and knowledge-enhancing partnerships, have all combined to give Nokia seamless innovation from concept to customer. Nokia's shareholder returns outpaced those of the rest of the mobile communications industry more than tenfold over the past six years, with its share price increasing from $1.26 in 1992 to $108 in 1998.

In industry after industry, innovation—whether breakthrough or continuous—that cuts across strategy, customer management, processes, and products and services has earned the companies able to harness it greater growth in value, and that value pays off for investors.

To be sure, the pivotal innovation factor for successful companies may vary, as we have seen. It may be the customer for a company such as Canon, or the supply chain and manufacturing for a Chrysler. But invariably, it is the boldest and most effective innovator that creates the most value.

If we compare Chrysler to Ford Motor Company, for example, we find a marked divergence in the approach to innovation. Ford has tended not to invest a lot in new products, and in the process it has produced some winners. Chrysler, on the other hand, has tended not only to its product pipeline but to innovations in its sourcing and partnering relationships and in its customer service and segmentation. The result: although Ford's market value has come close to that of its stodgy rival, General Motors, Chrysler's market capitalization has soared. Innovation has enabled Chrysler to change the rules of engagement in the auto industry and thereby create $3 billion of new shareholder value.

In sum, innovation builds customer satisfaction and brand loyalty; it helps keep employees satisfied and boosts a company's employee-retention rate; it increases partner satisfaction and preference; it wins more share of market and of mind—all of which translates into improved investor returns and glowing financial health, because the benefit of sustainable innovation leadership is consistently strong financial performance.

In our work with clients, in our research across industries, in our collaboration with the financial community, we are finding that next-generation businesses that innovate consistently and effectively—not just in products or services, but also in strategy and operations—are accorded a premium in the marketplace. These companies are more valuable to owners of their equity and debt, and more valuable as suppliers and customers of choice in their webs of commercial interaction.

Is there risk involved in committing a company to next-generation approaches, to setting out on the pathways leading to the innovation premium? Of course. Innovation implies risk. But to risk is to dare, and to dare is to seize the opportunity to succeed in previously unimagined ways. When innovation is properly conceived and managed, the reward repays the risk many times over. The consequence of consistent, enterprisewide growth and the ability to reward all stakeholders with the benefits of the innovation premium make it a risk well worth taking.

APPENDIX A

• •

Arthur D. Little
Global Survey on Innovation

*"Innovation in our company is viewed as a much
more critical business success factor than
it was just five years ago."*

Some 84 percent of the respondents to the Arthur D. Little Global Survey on Innovation strongly agree with this statement. Highly consistent with the experience of our clients around the world, this finding and others from this study confirm the degree to which innovation is stealing the spotlight from cost-cutting strategies such as restructuring and downsizing as business imperatives.

However, despite the race to innovate, less than 25 percent of the responding companies were happy with their current performance in innovation. Few believe that they have fully mastered the art of deriving business value from innovation.

This comprehensive study assessed the three primary types of innovation across regions and industries around the world:

Product/service innovation: *the creative development and commercialization of radically new products or services, often grounded in new technology and linked to unmet customer needs*

Process innovation: *the development of new ways of producing products or delivering services that lead to advantages in cost, or timeliness of delivery*

Business innovation: *the development of new businesses and new ways of conducting business that provide unbeatable competitive advantage*

In 1997 Arthur D. Little surveyed 669 companies in ten industries in the United States and Canada, Latin America, Europe, and the Asia-Pacific region. Respondents represented top-level management from chief executive officers and chief technology officers to business unit leaders, as well as functional management from R&D to marketing.

The survey asked four major groups of questions:

1. To what extent have companies shifted their strategic focus to innovation?
2. What are the most significant obstacles companies face in creating value from innovation?
3. What are the key success factors for deriving business value from innovation?
4. To what extent do leading companies today measure innovation success?

ARTHUR D. LITTLE RESEARCH IN INNOVATION

In 1991, Arthur D. Little conducted a survey of top management views on product innovation in the United States, Europe, and Japan. That study found that the top priority areas were making products better, cheaper, and faster and that a lack of appropriate resources presented the greatest obstacle to success.

Much changed in the years between the two surveys. Accelerated technical advances have created an explosion of information. Globalization has realigned the four key regions of economic activity. These and other factors have contributed to the emerging importance of other types of innovation in business. Arthur D. Little undertook this study to document the ways in which companies innovate and how they manage innovation around the world.

The four major regions represented in this study include the following (Figure A–1):

- United States and Canada
- Latin America (Brazil, Colombia, Mexico)
- Europe (Austria, Belgium, Denmark, Finland, France, Germany, Hungary, Italy, Norway, Spain, Sweden, Switzerland, United Kingdom)
- Asia-Pacific (Australia, Japan, Hong Kong, Korea, Singapore)

The respondents represented a solid cross-section of industries, including engineering/manufacturing, chemicals, information/media/electronics, consumer, pharmaceutical/health care, financial services, automotive, energy/utilities, metals/resources, and telecommunications.

Most questions were based on a five point scale in which a "1" was typically "low importance" or "little agreement" and a "5" "greatest importance" or

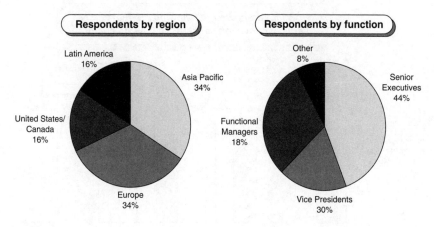

FIGURE A.1

"fully agree." The analysis typically groups "4"s and "5"s as "very important, strong agreement."

THE SURVEY RESULTS

As leading companies worldwide are shifting their focus from cost-cutting to growth, a renewed emphasis has been placed on the importance of innovation. In this new model, companies distinguish between product, service, process, and business innovation. This survey details four key findings:

1. Companies are placing high strategic priority on innovation but few feel that they are effective innovators today.
2. The two most significant obstacles to creating value are aligning innovation activities with strategy and operating effective cross-functional innovation processes.
3. Six key success factors appear to be most crucial to improving innovation performance.
4. Innovation performance can be measured, and those companies that do measure it derive the greatest value from their innovation activities.

Companies are placing high strategic priority on innovation, but few feel that they are effective innovators today. The survey reveals that innovation has significantly increased in importance over the last five years. However, few

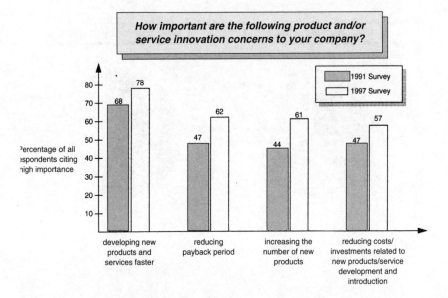

FIGURE A.2   Increase in importance of key product/service innovation concerns (1991–1997)

companies feel that their innovation capability is where it needs to be to succeed in the marketplace. This finding suggests two essential implications:

- Focusing on cost-cutting alone is insufficient to drive sustained business success in the future.
- There is ample opportunity for companies to gain competitive advantage through a concentrated effort at mastering the innovation process.

Innovation is strategically important.
Since our 1991 global survey on innovation, the importance of specific product innovation concerns has increased significantly (Figure A–2).

More than 80 percent of the respondents to the 1997 survey strongly agreed that innovation is viewed in their companies as a much more critical business success factor than it was five years ago (Figure A–3).

Agreement across industries varies considerably, given different maturities and life cycles. For example, as many as 60–80 percent of the respondents from the pharmaceuticals, consumer, and financial services industries compared with 25–40 percent in engineering/manufacturing, information/media/electronics, and metals/resources strongly agreed on the increasing importance of innovation as a key business success factor (Figure A–4).

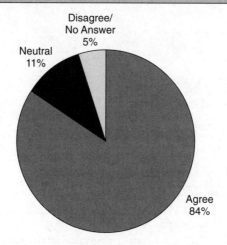

To what extent do you agree with this statement?

"Innovation is viewed as a much more critical business success factor than it was five years ago."

Disagree/
No Answer
5%

Neutral
11%

Agree
84%

FIGURE A.3   Innovation priority

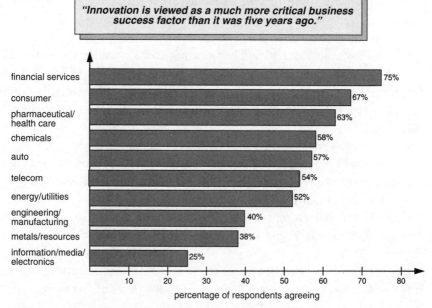

To what extent do you agree with this statement?

"Innovation is viewed as a much more critical business success factor than it was five years ago."

Industry	Percentage
financial services	75%
consumer	67%
pharmaceutical/health care	63%
chemicals	58%
auto	57%
telecom	54%
energy/utilities	52%
engineering/manufacturing	40%
metals/resources	38%
information/media/electronics	25%

percentage of respondents agreeing

FIGURE A.4   Innovation priority by industry

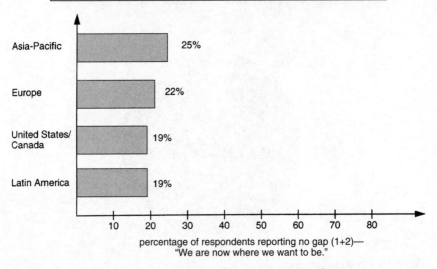

FIGURE A.5 Consolidated product/service, process, business-innovation gap by region

This surprising result may be explained by the fact that the information/media/electronics industries have traditionally relied on innovation to gain or maintain their leadership in an industry in which product/service life cycles are drastically shortening. They have not seen innovation increasing in importance because for them it has always been of the highest importance. Similarly, engineering and manufacturing industries that have reached the maturity stage before other industries also realized earlier the need to innovate.

Few companies have satisfactory innovation performance.

Despite the broad recognition of the importance of innovation for business success, few companies claim highly effective innovation performance. In our survey less than a quarter of the respondents claimed that they had little or no gap between their current innovation performance and the level they need to succeed in the marketplace, with surprisingly little variation by region (Figure A–5).

Likewise, no more than 40 percent of the respondents in any one industry surveyed felt that their company's innovation performance is where it needs to be to succeed in the marketplace (Figure A–6).

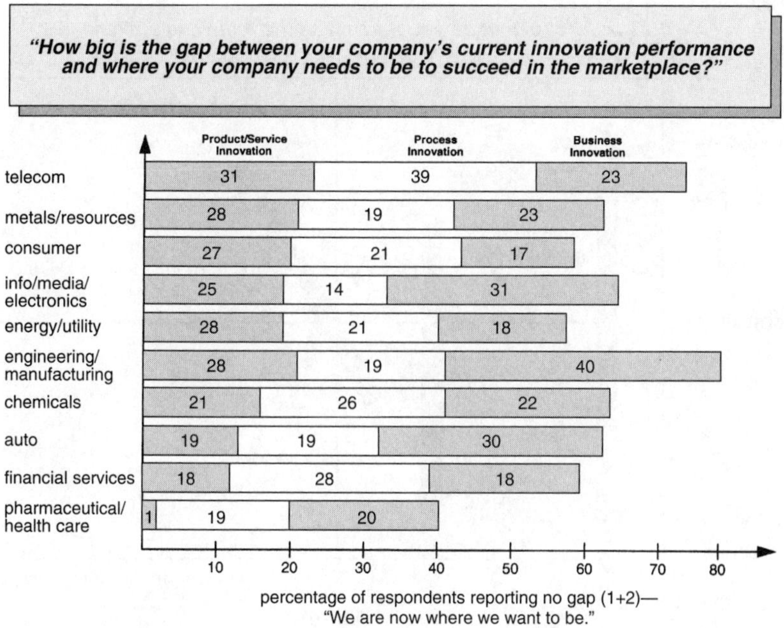

"How big is the gap between your company's current innovation performance and where your company needs to be to succeed in the marketplace?"

	Product/Service Innovation	Process Innovation	Business Innovation
telecom	31	39	23
metals/resources	28	19	23
consumer	27	21	17
info/media/electronics	25	14	31
energy/utility	28	21	18
engineering/manufacturing	28	19	40
chemicals	21	26	22
auto	19	19	30
financial services	18	28	18
pharmaceutical/health care	1	19	20

percentage of respondents reporting no gap (1+2)—
"We are now where we want to be."

FIGURE A.6   Product/service, process, business-innovation gap by industry

Implications for management.

"We've downsized, reengineered, and cost cut to the bone; now my stock price is stuck at $140. Where do we find the growth?" This type of question is common today.

Today and in the future, companies must explicitly focus their business strategies on growth through innovation; develop and align key processes for generating, cultivating, and launching new ideas; leverage the most appropriate resources from both internal and external sources; and rethink how they are organized to drive value creation across functions and between businesses. Those that do this effectively will realize unparalleled competitive advantage; those that do not may not survive into the next century.

One of the most significant obstacles to creating value is aligning innovation activities with strategy. There are significant obstacles that can limit the success of deriving value from innovation. Companies undertaking major innovation initiatives today struggle with fostering a culture that thrives on generating and capturing new ideas from a variety of sources. Executing downstream development processes is a continuing challenge, as is gathering the needed intelligence to make effective decisions about new ideas and products.

Respondents to our survey indicated that the top five obstacles actually reflect back to strategy and decision making, as shown in Figure A–8.

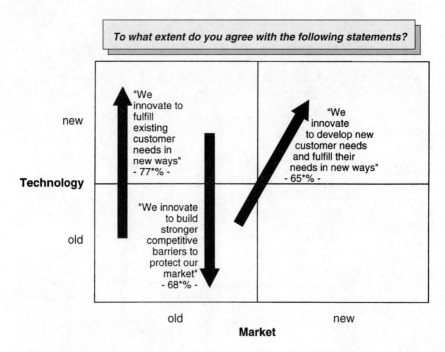

FIGURE A.7   Why innovate?

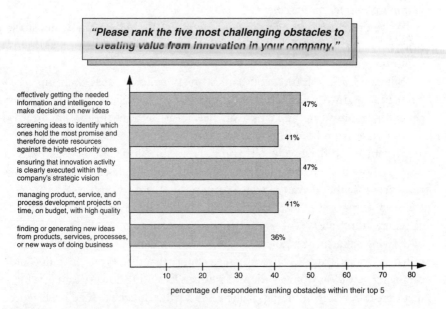

FIGURE A.8   Prevalence of top innovation obstacles

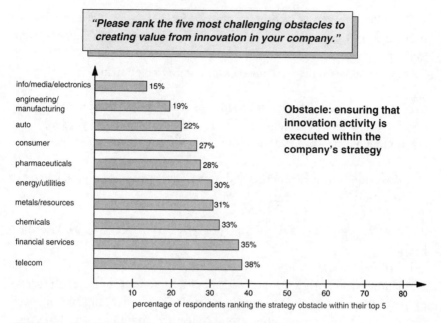

FIGURE A.9 Prevalence of strategic-related obstacles by industry

The data suggest what our experience with clients corroborates: that all companies struggle with similar themes when it comes to innovation. However, the importance of the obstacles varies by industry and, of course, by company (Figure A–9).

In the 1991 survey the biggest obstacles were resource-related: finding skilled leaders and managers, acquiring staff with appropriate skills, and effectively getting needed information and intelligence. The shift to strategy suggests that companies have realized the importance of driving innovation within the context of the businesses' strategy. Innovation not aligned with strategy can cause chaos and poor results.

To be successful, innovation has to be driven by a focused and shared vision of the company's future. We often find that companies with only a superficial understanding of long-term scenarios have difficulties in deciding where to go, rarely make decisions on their long-term strategic options, and therefore cannot achieve their innovation potential. Idea generation and idea ranking is therefore more difficult, as the survey confirms.

Overcoming these strategic obstacles is not a complicated task, once a company has crafted its strategy and decided to adopt an innovation focus— which suggests that the real challenge is overcoming the cultural issues.

Given the importance of product and service innovation, we also asked respondents how important *specific* product/service innovation concerns were to their company.

On a global basis, the top four concerns were the following:

- improving margin from our products and services (82 percent)
- increasing the sales volume of our products and services (79 percent)
- getting our new products and services to the market on time as planned (78 percent)
- developing our new products and services faster from concept to market introduction (78 percent)

On an industry basis, these top concerns vary somewhat, as described below:

Increasing the sales volume of our products and services.

All industries clearly are concerned about sales volume; however, the greatest percentage of respondents from companies in pharmaceuticals, financial services, and telecommunications were concerned about this aspect of product and service development.

Improving the margin from our products and services.

Respondents from all industries also placed high importance on improving margins, with the largest percentage from the chemicals industry (90 percent rating this as high importance) and the least from pharmaceuticals (76 percent rating as high importance).

Developing our new products and services faster from concept to market introduction.

The importance of development speed varied the most across industries, reflecting the broad set of companies represented in the survey. Not surprisingly, the smallest percent of respondents from companies in the metals/resources industries (59 percent) rated this concern as high importance. The highest percentage of respondents citing this concern as important came from pharmaceuticals (89 percent), automotive (89 percent), and telecommunications (89 percent), with engineering/manufacturing, information/media/electronics, and consumer not far behind.

Achieving high innovation performance requires careful alignment and execution of several key variables:

- strategy
- business processes
- resources (staff, facilities, equipment)
- organization (structure and culture)

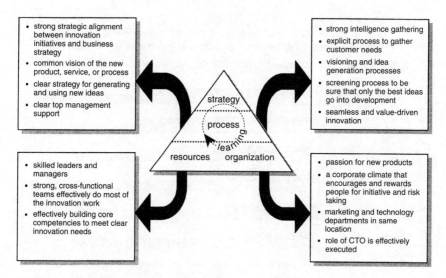

FIGURE A.10   High-performance business innovation key success factors

Expanding upon these variables yields a model of key success factors:

Further survey analysis identified six key success factors that are most crucial to improving innovation performance:

- clear top management support and commitment
- effectively executed role of chief technology officer (CTO)
- skilled leaders and managers
- marketing and technology departments in the same location
- seamless and value-driven innovation process
- visioning and idea generation processes

Although some of these factors seem obvious, many companies lack a clear vision, aligned processes, or perhaps effective organizations or resources and therefore are not well-positioned to leverage innovation effectively across their businesses.

In fact, most of the survey respondents agreed that these factors can be highly effective in helping their companies derive business value from their innovation activities. Unfortunately, relatively few companies believe that they actually possess these key success factors to a great extent, as shown in figure A–11.

Analysis of the data suggests that a useful way to approach some of the softer sides of business management is to consider the important factors that lead to success, in which success is defined as driving business value creation

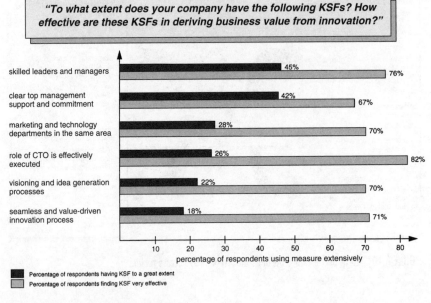

FIGURE A.11   Innovation: key success factors

(increased shareholder equity, higher stock price, more return on investment, and so on). The six important innovation key success factors may be defined as follows:

1. *Clear top management support and commitment:* The chief executive officer and other business leaders set the tone for the organization. They lead the creation and execution of business strategy and they affect the culture and behavior of the organization. Chief executives need to communicate explicitly the importance of innovation; be willing to invest for the longer term; and be tolerant of failure in the spirit of developing and launching new products, services, and businesses, in order to foster a climate conducive to strong innovation.

2. *Effectively executed role of chief technology officer (CTO):* Whatever the title, a management sponsor with executive-level decision-making authority or influence over the company's technology assets is critical. In the rush to reduce costs, many companies have significantly reduced or eliminated central research and development in favor of business unit-based development centers. While this may have improved customer focus, it often has a negative effect on innovation—without an enterprise view of

a firm's technology assets, companies may miss key opportunities arising between business units or sectors.

3. *Skilled leaders and managers:* Effective innovation is impossible without critical marketing, technology, production skills, and leadership capability. Many large corporations today are facing a "hollowing-out" through early retirements and other measures; companies are realizing that they lack the fundamental skills required to bring new products and services to the market.

4. *Marketing and technology departments in the same location:* Technology and marketing departments rarely communicate effectively. Technology says, "If marketing could only tell us what they want, we could produce it" and marketing says, "if technology could only tell us what they can make, we could sell it!" Logistics can exacerbate the problem, since the physical separation of the functions dramatically reduces the chance for the strong cooperation and clear communication that is critical to successful innovation.

5. *Seamless and value-driven innovation process:* By its very nature, innovation involves an enterprisewide cooperative spirit. The process needs to be seamless in that the flow of information, material, and activities must pass among functions, groups, or other boundaries smoothly and quickly with no losses along the way. Similarly, it must be *value-driven* in that everyone's work must be well-aligned with the ultimate objective and focused on the right activities that lead to value creation.

6. *Visioning and idea generation processes:* Bringing new products and services to market, implementing alternative production processes, or executing new business models often requires explicit techniques for creating a vision of future possibilities and generating specific ideas. Companies are depending on countless approaches to the "fuzzy front end" of the innovation process, and, as our survey has shown, these activities are very important to effective innovation.

Innovation performance can be measured; those companies that do so have smaller gaps in deriving value from their innovation activities. Almost every company employs specific performance measures to gauge progress. As we have seen, product, service, process, and business innovation plays a direct role in driving business performance. However, until now relatively few companies specifically have measured the effectiveness of their innovation activity, despite enormous investments in technology, marketing, and so on. In our experience those few companies that do specifically use key innovation measures are much more likely to derive business value over time from their efforts.

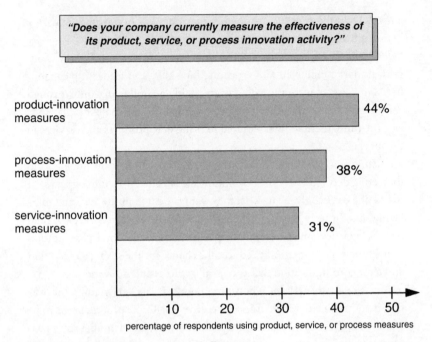

"Does your company currently measure the effectiveness of its product, service, or process innovation activity?"

product-innovation measures — 44%

process-innovation measures — 38%

service-innovation measures — 31%

percentage of respondents using product, service, or process measures

FIGURE A.12 Overall use of measurement of effectiveness

Indeed, our survey results support this assertion. Fewer than 50 percent of the respondents across the globe use product or process innovation measures, and only about one-third employ service innovation measures (Figure A–12).

On a global basis those companies that do use product or service measures are statistically more likely to belong to the group believing that they had little or no product or service innovation gap—i.e., those feeling that their companies are where they need to be to succeed in the marketplace (Figure A–13). Despite the potential for inconsistency in self-reported performance, our experience in working with clients around the world supports this supposition: *applying specific innovation measures increases the value of your innovation activity.*

What kind of measures tend to be used, and how effective are they? The survey classifies measures in four categories:

1. Lagging: These incur a significant time delay after the key action occurs and are typically based on financial results.
2. Real time: These are 'in-process' and typically relate to the timelines of completion of the activity.

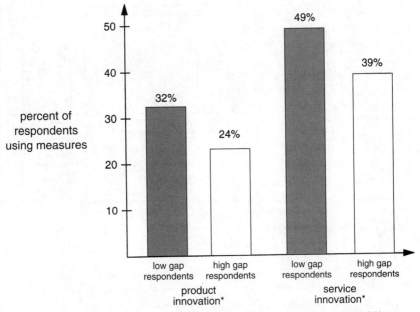

*Interpretation: For product innovation, you are statistically more likely to fall into the low innovation gap group if you use innovation measures.

FIGURE A.13 Significance of measurement

3. Leading: These indicators attempt to predict success by measuring cultural or climate-related factors.
4. Learning: These typically access the rate of improvement in a key measure.

Figure A–14 reflects the top three measures used in each category.

Regional differences in the extent of use of different categories of measures at this aggregate level are insignificant. However, some statistical differences emerge in the extent of use of specific measures across regions within each category.

Lagging indicator usage.

Common indicators such as revenue, profit margins, and market share are fairly widely used in all regions (57–70 percent) as shown in Figure A–15.

A key lagging indicator that is becoming more common is percentage of revenues from new products or services; in fact, companies in the Asia-Pacific (49 percent) region tend to be more likely to use this measure than companies in Europe (38 percent) or Latin America (36 percent). However, these measures tend to be difficult to define.

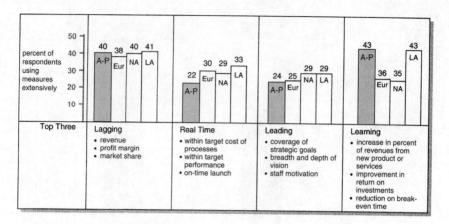

FIGURE A.14   Top innovation measures

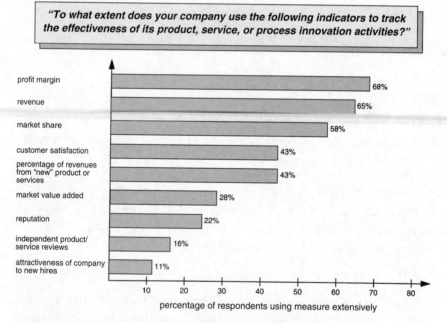

"To what extent does your company use the following indicators to track the effectiveness of its product, service, or process innovation activities?"

- profit margin — 68%
- revenue — 65%
- market share — 58%
- customer satisfaction — 43%
- percentage of revenues from "new" product or services — 43%
- market value added — 28%
- reputation — 22%
- independent product/service reviews — 16%
- attractiveness of company to new hires — 11%

percentage of respondents using measure extensively

FIGURE A.15   Use of lagging indicators as measurement of effectiveness

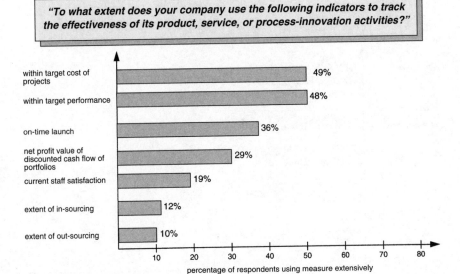

FIGURE A.16 Use of real-time indicators as measurement of effectiveness

Real-time indicator usage.

- Application of real time indicators varies considerably across regions, as shown in Figure A–16.
- The Americas (United States, Canada, Latin America) tend to use "on time launch" more extensively than Asia-Pacific.
- Europe tends to use "net profit value of discounted cash flow of portfolio" more extensively.
- Europe focuses on "within target cost of projects" more than Asia-Pacific and "within target performance" more than Latin America.
- Asia-Pacific applies "current staff satisfaction" significantly more extensively than any of the other regions (37 percent vs. 13–18 percent).

Leading indicator usage.

The most difficult to apply, leading indicators are, not surprisingly, used the least extensively by all regions, as shown in Figure A–17. Some interesting regional differences in application of specific measures include the following:

- Latin America employs "staff motivation" significantly more extensively than Asia-Pacific or Europe (36 percent vs. 23 percent or 24 percent, respectively).

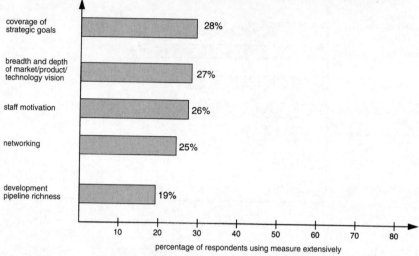

"To what extent does your company use the following indicators to track the effectiveness of its product, service, or process-innovation activities?"

coverage of strategic goals — 28%
breadth and depth of market/product/technology vision — 27%
staff motivation — 26%
networking — 25%
development pipeline richness — 19%

percentage of respondents using measure extensively

FIGURE A.17   Use of leading indicators as measurement of effectiveness

- Latin America and Europe use "coverage of strategic goals" more frequently than Asia-Pacific (32–34 percent vs. 22 percent).
- Asia-Pacific, Europe, and Latin America measure "networking" more extensively than the United States or Canada.

Learning indicator usage.

Learning indicators typically reflect rate of improvement in specific parameters. Increasingly, leading companies today are adopting programs and processes to augment organizational learning. In parallel, they are beginning to develop learning indicators to assess improvement, particularly in the innovation area. Companies in Asia-Pacific appear to be particularly advanced in this area, as shown in Figure A–18.

- Asia-Pacific companies use "increase in percent of revenues from new products or services" more extensively than their counterparts in either Europe or the United States and Canada (54 percent vs. 42 percent or 43 percent).
- Asia-Pacific companies also use "reduction in break-even time" more extensively than their counterparts in Europe, the United States or Canada (34 percent vs. 25 percent or 15 percent).

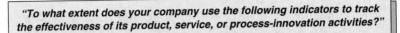

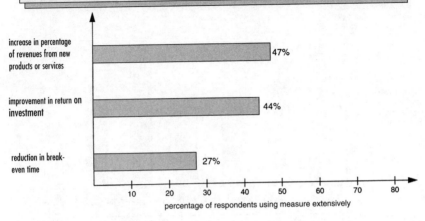

FIGURE A.18   Use of learning indicators as measurement of effectiveness

The data reveal that innovation is a strategic priority, but few companies do it well. Key success factors exist, but there are lots of obstacles to overcome. Innovation indicators can be applied, but solid measures are hard to implement. Our survey results suggest that four conditions must be met for an organization to become an innovation powerhouse:

1. *Secure senior management commitment to a corporate innovation strategy.* Corporate or business strategy is the important starting point for improving a company's innovation performance. Some 82 percent of the respondents worldwide believed to a great extent that a top management commitment to and focus on increasing its organization's innovative ability could lead to significant bottom line results over and above typical cost-cutting and reengineering initiatives, because, in the words of our respondents, "Innovation is the driver of growth."

2. *Develop and implement an innovation process that spans the value chain.* Innovation is indeed a business process, perhaps not as linear as, say, an order entry process; nevertheless it is a collection of key business activities with a starting point, an ending point, and a flow of knowledge across functions. Somewhat more than half of the respondents to our survey strongly agreed that innovation is now specifically managed as a business process.

   In fact, leading companies today no longer let innovation just happen; they employ disciplined techniques such as visioning, technology road-

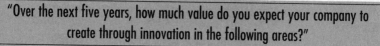

"Over the next five years, how much value do you expect your company to create through innovation in the following areas?"

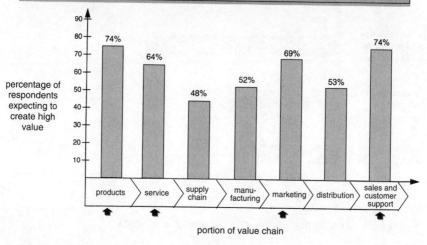

FIGURE A.19   Where to innovate in the value chain by region

mapping, and core competency analysis, etc., according to 55 percent of the survey respondents.

In addition, they expect to create high value from innovation in a number of steps in the value chain, particularly in products, services, marketing, and sales/customer support. (Figure A–19).

3. *Obtain the best resources from within your firm and beyond, to drive the process.* In our work with clients, we have found that nearly every company has strong resources that could be better channeled to drive innovation performance. Sometimes, it's the creative mavericks who have all but given up their outspoken ways, frustrated beyond belief by the lack of change. Or perhaps it is the fortuitous partnership with a local university or supplier that could energize a product line but instead is mired in the legal department, crippled by such key issues as ownership of intellectual property.

Effective innovation requires a very broad definition of a firm's resources, an explicit process for managing partnerships for both in-sourcing and out-sourcing of technology, and finally, a commitment to invest for the future.

4. *Transform your organization's structure and culture to nurture and drive high innovation performance.* Organizational structure and culture can be the strongest lever management has to improve innovation performance, and the most difficult to transform. Even the best-laid plans will fail if the values and visions for an innovative culture are not shared. Careful attention must be paid to the impact of key innovation decisions. In the survey we identified several approaches that we consider in helping clients find ways to overcome organizational and cultural barriers to innovation.

The four approaches that were found to be most highly effective are the following:

1. *Walk the talk.* Develop innovation leadership abilities in senior and middle management and encourage them to lead by example. A shared vision among management for innovation in the company will foster common values that guide actions, and reduce the need for specifying and supervising the actions of others.
2. *Provide training in cross-functional team skills.* Boundaries within the organization should be permeable to encourage cross-functional teams which will further the development of a seamless innovation process across the enterprise.
3. *Reward teams collectively for team accomplishments.* Rewards can influence behavior. Recognizing team accomplishments through means other than financial incentives (i.e. positive feedback, public appraisal) reinforces the common vision and values of the innovative culture.
4. *Incorporate innovation measures into performance reviews.* Performance should be measured against ambitious innovation targets tied to collaboration and corporate innovation vision.

CONCLUSIONS

There is no single "right way" to innovate. Innovation is indeed a complex and sometimes ambiguous activity that is heavily influenced by corporate cultures and even individual personalities. All companies (and most people) have their own vision of where and how to innovate. Despite these differences this study has demonstrated that there is the near-unified belief that innovation is the engine for growth and the driver for value for the future. There is an understanding that innovation must be tied to corporate strategy in order to be realized. There is an appreciation for the tremendous complexity of innovation management, but also an acknowledgement that it can and should be managed. There is an awakening to methods of measuring innovation in ways that reveal its value to stakeholders and that drive organizational behavior to capture this value. There is an acceptance that effective innovation involves not only products, but processes, services, and business across the entire value chain and extended enterprise. And there is the realization that most companies are still learning how to manage innovation within their organization. In fact, those who have ceased to learn, have ceased to innovate.

APPENDIX B

• •

A Survey of Financial Analysts' Perceptions of Innovation

As part of our ongoing series of studies on innovations in business, Arthur D. Little recently conducted a study of buy-side and sell-side analysts on how they define innovation and the impact on corporate performance. In an effort to better understand the implications of the study, Arthur D. Little asked David Michaelson & Associates, Inc., to prepare an analysis of the data collected in this project.

The specific objectives of this research were to determine:

- factors most associated with innovation
- how analysts define innovation
- the overall importance of innovation in corporate performance
- impact of innovation on shareholder value
- companies considered most innovative

Research Method

Questionnaires were sent by fax to a cross-section of buy-side and sell-side analysts throughout the United States by Arthur D. Little. These questionnaires were returned directly to ADL for data tabulation and analysis. Approximately 450 questionnaires were distributed, and thirty-seven completed and usable questionnaires were returned for analysis. This represented a return rate of approximately eight percent.

Reading Notes:

- Percentages read across when percent signs appear in left-hand columns.
- Percentages read down when percent signs are at the top of columns.
- Throughout the report, the minus sign signifies any value less than 1 percent.

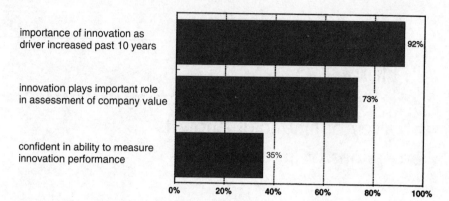

FIGURE B.1 Agreement with statements about innovation

- Where percentages add to more than 100 percent (or total shown), it is due to multiple answers.
- Where percentages add up to less than the total or less than 100 percent, the differences are due to the exclusion of the "don't knows" and "no answers."
- Sometimes, where Figures do not add to the totals shown, differences are due to "rounding" the percentages.
- All bases shown are unweighted.

Findings

1. *Few analysts are confident they can measure innovation.* They almost universally recognize that innovation is key in assessing a company's value (73 percent) and that its importance has increased over the past decade (92 percent). Nonetheless, only one in three (35 percent) analysts claim confidence in measuring how this innovation affects a company's performance.

2. *While few know how to measure innovation, almost all believe innovation increases shareholder value.* Ninety-five percent of analysts believe companies that are more innovative can earn a higher shareholder premium.

   The reason behind this belief that innovation deserves a shareholder premium is that innovation is important in sustaining a company's performance or growth (23 percent). Innovation is also important in differentiating companies from one another and giving them a competitive

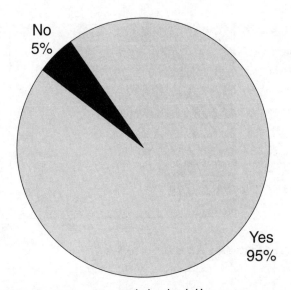

FIGURE B.2   More innovative companies earn higher shareholder premiums.

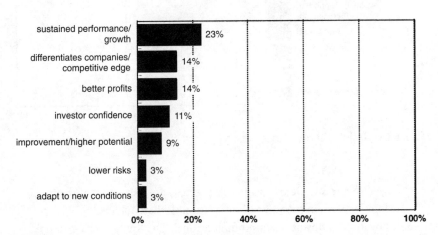

FIGURE B.3   Why innovation deserves shareholder premiums

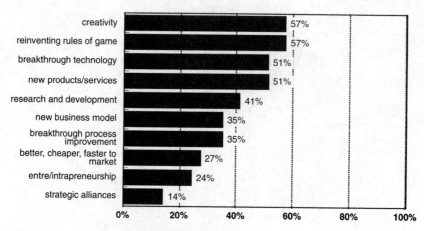

FIGURE B.4 Items most associated with innovation in business

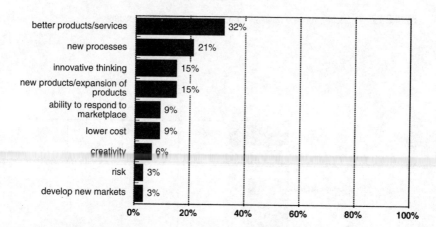

FIGURE B.5 Definition of innovation—open-ended

edge (14 percent). Better profits (14 percent) are also a part of the mix in helping to explain the value of innovation to shareholders.

3. Innovation in business is multidimensional. The four aspects of innovation that are most commonly associated with business innovations are "creativity" (57 percent), "reinventing the rules of the game" (57 percent), breakthrough technology" (51 percent), and "new products and services" (51 percent).

Surprisingly, research and development appears much less likely to be seen as a center of innovation. Nonetheless, 41 percent of analysts still associate this function with business innovations.

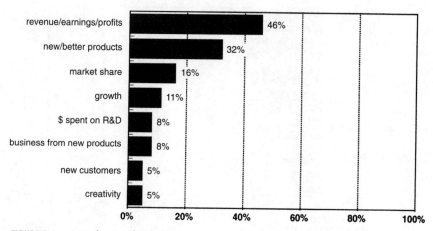

FIGURE B.6 Key indicators of innovation

Changes in process and new business models are seen as part of innovation by 35 percent of analysts. Increasing speed to market and entrepreneurship are typically seen as less likely to be a part of innovation.

4. While new products and creativity are significant elements of innovation, profit and earnings are the key indicator.

Almost half (46 percent) of analysts surveyed feel that revenue, earnings, or profits are the key indicator of innovation. One in three look to the product pipeline as another indicator.

However, while profits are important, market share is considerably less likely to be considered an indicator of innovation. Only 16 percent look to this as an indicator. Even fewer (11 percent) consider growth as an indicator of innovation.

5. Information technology and electronics are the companies most associated with innovation.

Four in ten (41 percent) analysts look to these companies as leaders in innovation. Meanwhile, 30 percent name companies in the manufacturing sector as being innovative. One in four (22 percent) believe energy is a center of innovation with 19 percent saying that retailing is leading the way.

SAMPLE RELIABILITY

In traditional survey research error rates for responses to particular questions are based on a model that presumes two factors: an infinite universe of potential re-

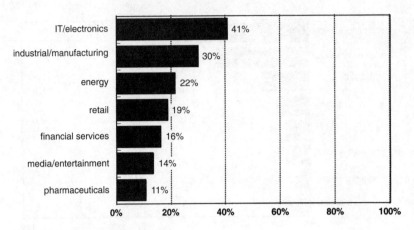

FIGURE B.7   Most innovative companies

spondents and questions that are asked of nonexperts. If that were the case in this study, the sample of thirty-seven analysts would be subject to extreme variations as noted in Figure B.7. Using this traditional statistical model, if we consider a result of 60 percent based on the total sample these analysts *(N = 37),* we would be 95 percent sure that the true result is within the range of nineteen percentage points above or below the sample result (that is, within the range of 41 percent to 79 percent).

However, in this study, the small sample actually represents a high proportion of the overall universe of potential respondents. By comparison, in order for a national public opinion poll to have the same proportion of its universe included in this study it would require a sample of millions of respondents. Consequently, the true error rate for this study is considerably lower and the reliance on the expert opinions included in this findings reinforces the reliability of the results.

NOTES

CHAPTER 1

1   "Get too hot . . . to cool down": Porter, Cole. Too Darn Hot. Kiss Me Kate. 13 January 1949. Record.

5   "A lone wolf among Japanese companies":

5   "Advanced technology development . . . our strategic thrust": Takahashi, Toru. [CANON]

6   "In the past . . . this group's activities": Linden, Kaj.

6–7   Nokia Case Study. Interview by Ronald Jonash. Tape recording, 26 August 1998.

6   "We learned to . . . able to garner": Ibid.

8   "Ford and General . . . entirely the opposite": Moore, Tom. Interview by Ronald Jonash and Maurice Coyle, tape recording, Detroit, Mi., 22 July 1998.

8   "We explain the . . . with other parts": Ibid.

11   "We continue to . . . a valuable experience": Clarke, Chris. Telephone conversation with Ronald Jonash and Maurice Coyle, 30 April 1998.

11   "We reward how . . . that particular metric": Arya, Atul. Telephone conversation with Ronald Jonash and Maurice Coyle, 30 April 1998.

CHAPTER 3

25   "We have no fear of cannibalism": Takahashi, Toru. [CANON]

29   "We do not . . . we have shareholders": [Millennium]

29   "We get more . . . pay the premium": Pavia, Michael. Interview by Ronald Jonash and Martha Lawler, tape recording, 21 October 1998.

29   "They pay us . . . builds on itself": Pavia, Michael.

Interview by Ronald Jonash and Martha Lawler, tape recording, 21 October 1998.

30   "Who will take . . . these platforms further": Holtzman, Steven. Interview by Ronald Jonash and Martha Lawler, tape recording, 21 October 1998.

32   "There is no . . . is an investment": Pavia, Michael. Interview by Ronald Jonash and Martha Lawler, tape recording, 21 October 1998.

37   "We intend to . . . and multifunction systems": [CANON]

CHAPTER 5

55   "Well, the iceberg survived": Moore, Tom, "Interview," 98.
59   "They don't drop the ball": Moore, Tom, "Interview," 98.
59   "We get messed . . . four levels below": Ibid.
59   "Now that you . . . make any difference": Ibid.
61   "There's almost nothing . . . a team process": Ibid.
63   "Before we even . . . invent it together": Ibid.
63   "The only leaks we at Chrysler have had are from employees who quit . . . We control the package, and the content of the features, and the weight, and the cost margins": Ibid.

CHAPTER 6

72   "To move beyond . . . and technology engine": Smith, Dr. Greg [ALCOA]
72   "We need more . . . pull and engagement": Belda, Alain. [ALCOA]
72–73 "The key to . . . innovation and development": Smith, Dr. Greg [ALCOA]
73   "This understanding of . . . with a valued partner": Smith, Dr. Greg [ALCOA]
76   "We each consider . . . make of it": Kagermann, Dr. Hermann.[SAP]
76   "Is to engage . . . technology and innovation": Lederman, Frank. [ALCOA]
76–77 "We need to . . . to our customers": Perez, Bill. [S.C. JOHNSON]
77   "We have set . . . a different company": Mulcahy [Eveready Battery Company's Energizer unit]
77   "Product innovation is . . . improve our products": McClanathan, Joe. [Eveready Battery Company's Energizer unit]

83 "The research-and-development group . . . acted as an interceptor": Rosenthal, Art. Interview by Ronald Jonash and Maurice
Coyle, 25 February 1998.

83 "Other people saw . . . for other businesses": Rosenthal, Art. Interview by Ronald Jonash and Maurice Coyle, 25 February 1998.

84 "They are the . . . works extremely well": Rosenthal, Art. Interview
by Ronald Jonash and Maurice Coyle, 25 February 1998.

89–90 "The people in the different plants to know who to call when they
have a problem . . . We can immediately start the post-acquisition
integration work and transfer technology and best practices from
us to them and vice versa": Roddy, Jerry. [Alcoa]

90 "These technology transfers . . . to work on": Sibly, John.[Alcoa]

90 "Once the gaps . . . computer-enhanced ideation": Smith, Dr.
Greg. [ALCOA]

90 "The ingot network . . . our innovation efforts": Smith, Dr. Greg.
[ALCOA]

CHAPTER 7

93 "Learning is at . . . rapidly and fully": Browne, John [BRITISH PE-
TROLEUM]

94 "The top management . . . transferring the lessons": Browne, John
[BRITISH PETROLEUM]

97 "You can change . . . of the enterprise": ": Clarke, Chris. Telephone
conversation with Ronald Jonash and Maurice Coyle, 30 April
1998.

97 "You can learn . . . All are crucial": Browne, John. [BRITISH PE-
TROLEUM]

102 "You want to . . . what you do": BRITISH PETROLEUM

102 "Tomorrow's most successful . . . capacity to learn": Shell Oil

102 "Technology designed for . . . customers and suppliers": Shell Oil

CHAPTER 8

106 "The corporation of the future": John A. Byrne, "The Corporation
of the Future," Business Week, August 31, 1998, p. 102.

108 "Amazing things happen . . . judgment and discretion": Kelleher,
Herb. [SOUTHWEST AIRLINES]

109   "If you want to have an innovative enterprise, you need people to be comfortable with taking risks . . . Old style is to look for somebody to blame": Arya, Atul. Telephone conversation with Ronald Jonash and Maurice Coyle, 30 April 1998.

109–110 "The object is . . . to be creative": John F. Welch Jr

INDEX

· ·

Academic researchers, relationships
  with, 49
Alcoa, 3, 9–10, 71–74, 89, 90
Alcoa Production System (APS), 73
Arthur D. Little Global Survey on
  Innovation, xii, 115–136
  concerns, innovation, of
    respondents in, 118(fig.), 124
  management in, implications for,
    121
  on measuring performance,
    127–133
  on obstacles to creating value,
    121–123
  on organizational structure, 135
  on process, 127, 133–134
  on resources, 133, 134
  on satisfaction with performance,
    120, 121(fig.)
  on strategy, 118–119, 121, 123,
    133
  success factors reported in,
    125–127
  on types of innovation, 123
Arthur D. Little Survey of Financial
  Analysts', xi-xii, 137–142
  findings of, 138–141, 142(fig.)
  objectives of, 137

reliability of, 141–142
research methods of, 137–138
Arya, Atul, 11, 109

Belda, Alain, 72
Boston Scientific, 3, 81–84
British Petroleum Company (BP),
  10–11, 13, 93–96, 109
Browne, John, 93–94, 97
Business cycle, 1
Business model. See Next-
  generation business model
Business Week, 106

Canon, Inc., 5, 23–25, 37, 39, 105
Chief development officer (CDO),
  9, 10, 75–77, 88
Chief learning officer (CLO), 10
Chrysler Corporation
  networks at, 61, 79–80
  platforms at, 23
  resources at, use of, 7–8, 55
  shareholder returns, 56(fig.)
  suppliers, partnering with, 7–8,
    58–60, 63–64
Cisco Systems, 62, 106–107
Clarke, Chris, 11
Competency platform, 3